Y0-BDQ-112

Satirical Dictionary
OF VOLTAIRE

EDITED, ILLUSTRATED, AND IN A

NEW ENGLISH VERSION BY

Paul McPharlin

THE PETER PAUPER PRESS
Mount Vernon, New York

PQ
2075
1946

COPYRIGHT 1945, 1946 • PETER PAUPER PRESS

32828

JENKINS LD COMPANY
COLBY JUNIOR COLLEGE
NEW LONDON, NEW HAMPSHIRE

Preliminaries

EDITOR'S NOTE: *The articles in this* Satirical Dictionary, *more of them than there were in the first edition* (1945), *do not suffer from the condensation they have undergone; instead they have been brought into line with Voltaire's original intention. His rapier-thrusts first appeared as* Questions on the Encyclopedia, *then were reprinted as* Reason by Alphabet, *both small pocket volumes. After his death, however, they were padded with many of his other papers into the eight-volume* Philosophical Dictionary, *not so much a blunderbuss as an omnibus. It has been tempting to add a word here and there, by way of compensation for the many words deleted from the more prolix and untidy writings; but these added words, if not Voltaire's, are within the vocabulary of his intention.*

PAUL McPHARLIN

INTRODUCTION: The Philosophical Dictionary *is Voltaire's principal essay in philosophy, though not a sustained work. The miscellaneous articles he contributed to Diderot's* Encyclopedia *which compose this* Dictionary *embody a mass of scholarly research, criticism, and speculation, lit up with pungent sallies at the formal and tyrannous ecclesiasticism of the period and the bases of belief on which it stood.*

These short studies reflect every phase of Voltaire's sparkling genius. Though some of the views enunciated in them are now universally held, and others have become obsolete through extended knowledge, they were startlingly new when Voltaire, at peril of freedom and reputation, spread them before the people of all civilized nations, who read them still with their first charm of style and substance.

OLIVER H. G. LEIGH

PREFACE: *This book does not require continuous reading; but wherever one opens it, matter for reflection can be found. The most satisfactory books are those of which the reader is part author: he can develop the ideas therein presented, correct their errors, and bolster from the stuff of his own mind their shortcomings.*

Only enlightened people can read this book. The ordinary man will get nothing from it; philosophy is not for him. Those who feel that certain truths must be hidden from the masses need have no cause for alarm. The masses do not read. They work all week and drink all their day off. And so, as books of philosophy are made only for philosophers, every conscientious man must try to be a philosopher, without deluding himself that he is one.

The information in this alphabet is extracted from the best standard works; and if the author does not always mention his sources, which he hopes will be recognized, he must not be suspected of wishing to take the credit for other people's work. He himself remains anonymous, and takes the position of the Gospel, "Let not thy left hand know what thy right hand doeth."

[VOLTAIRE]

4

The Contents

SATIRICAL
DICTIONARY
Voltaire

Adam

WHY was there such profound secrecy about Adam throughout the habitable earth, save in Palestine, until the time when Hebrew scriptures began to be known in Alexandria?

Such is the mystery of Providence, that the father and mother of the human race might have been totally unknown to their descendants — for the names of Adam and Eve are to be found in no ancient author of Greece, Rome, Persia, or Syria, nor even of the Arabs until almost the time of Mahomet—had not it been God's pleasure that the origin of the great family of the world be concealed from all but the smallest and most unfortunate part of that family.

Nothing will here be said of Adam's second wife, Lilith, given him by the ancient rabbis. Very little family gossip has come down to us.

The pious Mme. de Bourignon was sure that Adam was a hermaphrodite, like the first men of the divine Plato. God had revealed a very intimate secret to her; but as I have not had the same revelation, I say nothing of the matter.

9

Adultery

THIS term is not heard in good company. We do not say, "Madame la Duchesse lives in adultery with Monsieur le Chevalier," or "Madame la Marquise has criminal relations with Monsieur l'Abbé." We say, "This week Monsieur l'Abbé is the lover of Madame la Marquise." Ladies discussing with their friends their adulteries remark, "I confess I'm rather fond of him." They used to confess that they felt "some esteem," but since the time when a certain housewife told her confessor that she had esteem for a high official, and he asked how many proofs of esteem there had been given, ladies of quality have esteemed no one—and gone but little to confession.

About the year 1764 a French judge was so unfortunate as to marry a woman who had been led astray by a priest, and who continued to waver of her own accord. He was obliged to leave her. Being, however, but forty and in lusty health, he needed a companion. Too scrupulous to seek another man's wife, and too fearful to consort with prostitutes, he pleaded earnestly with the Church:

"My wife erred and I am the one to suffer. A woman is necessary to me. Without one how can I keep my virtue? Yet you refuse her to me; I cannot marry another. You compel me either to take pleasure which you reprobate or consolation which you condemn. You force me to be a criminal.

"Your priests and monks may abstain from women if need be; I have no objections. It checks the increase in population. They deserve the

10

misfortune they have contrived for themselves. But I, a judge who serves mankind all day, have need of a little womankind at night."

Then there was the Countess D'Arcira of Portugal, a wife who made this plea before a junta: "The Gospels forbid adultery both to my husband and me. Well, it seems we'll both be damned together. He has been guilty of fifty infidelities—he gave my necklace to one woman, my earrings to another—and I have imitated him only once, and then with the handsomest young man in Lisbon. Must I then answer questions before a panel of men, any one of whom would lose no time in such nonsense if he were alone with me? Must I have this lovely hair cut off? Must I be confined with nuns who are not quite bright? Must I be deprived of the fortune I brought my husband so that he can go on seducing women and committing adulteries? I ask, is this justice?"

It would appear that, in order to assure a just verdict in an action for adultery, the jury should be composed of six men and six women, and—in the event of a tie — a hermaphrodite to cast the deciding vote.

St. Augustine, in his commentary on the Sermon on the Mount, tells this story: Septimus Acyndicus, proconsul of Syria, threw into prison a Christian of Antioch who was unable to pay the pound of gold he owed for taxes, and threatened him with death. His wife was promised by a wealthy man the necessary gold if she would lie with him. The wife hastened to inform her husband, who begged her to save his life even at this cost. She went through with the bargain, but the sack she received was filled not with gold but with earth. The husband, still unable to pay his

11

taxes, was on his way to the scaffold when the proconsul, hearing everything, paid the money from
his own coffers and gave the Christian couple the
estate from which the sack of earth had been
taken. St. Augustine does not pass judgment on
them.

A word on the paradox of the education we
give our daughters. They are taught to spare no
pains in pleasing; they learn every refinement of
the art. When they are trained to a fine degree we
punish them if they so much as venture to show
their accomplishments. What should we think
of a dancing master who, after drilling a pupil
for ten years, broke his leg when he found him
dancing?

Almanac

SUPPOSE that a philosopher should set out from
India, a man with common sense and no fixed
academic ideas — a rare thing, you may object,
among the educated in India and rare anywhere
else not too long ago—and meet a blockhead in
our part of the world—not so great a rarity. The
blockhead, in order to tell him something of our
arts and sciences, might give him one of those
almanacs got up by an astrologer, which sell
twenty thousand copies in a week. In them you
see the figure of a man surrounded by the signs
of the zodiac, with lines to indicate that Scales
influences his posterior, Ram his head, Fishes his
feet, and so on. The phases of the moon tell you
when you should take So-and-so's balm of life, or
somebody else's pills, and the days are shown
when you should be bled, cut your nails, wean

12

your children, put out seedings, sow, start on a journey, or break in new shoes. The man from India, seeing all this, would probably raise his eyebrows.

Then the simpleton might show the philosopher a few of our ceremonies — disapproved by the wise but tolerated because they amuse the people—and the traveler, seeing them, might take us for madmen, rather amusing nevertheless, and not really savage. He would write home to the president of the College of Benares that we have little brains, but that if His Paternity were to send some good professors out to us, they might, with the blessings of God, educate us.

It was just like this that our first missionaries, especially St. Francis Xavier, spoke of the people of India. They fell into even more serious errors in observing Indian customs, sciences, opinions, manners, and religion. The accounts which they sent to Europe were decidedly curious. Every image was a demon, every assembly of worship a black sabboth, every symbol a talisman, every Brahmin a sorcerer; and they deplored everything they saw. Nevertheless they hoped that their harvest would be abundant, and that they might labor effectually in the vineyard of the Lord—in a land where wine was unknown. Thus have people always judged not only distant lands, but their neighbors across the national border.

Animals

WHAT a pitiful and sorry thing to say that animals are mere mechanisms, bereft of understanding and feeling! What of the bird that builds its nest in a semicircle when attaching it to a wall, in a quarter circle when in a corner, and in a complete circle on a branch? What of the hunting dog that you train for three months; doesn't he know more than when you started?

Is it because I can speak to you that you judge me to have feeling, memory, and ideas? If I did not speak, and you saw me come in looking downcast, searching anxiously for a paper, opening the desk where I remember having shut it, then finding it and joyfully reading it, would you not judge that I felt distress and pleasure, that I had memory and understanding? Apply the same judgment to a dog that has lost its master, that goes searching him up and down every road, whimpering, that comes in and goes up and down stairs and from room to room, until it finds him at last in his study, and giving yelps of delight, jumps and caresses him.

Scholastics ask whether animals have a soul. I do not understand their question. A tree can pull the sap into its fibers and unfold the buds of its leaves and blossoms; does it have a soul? It has received certain faculties. Animals have those of feeling, memory, and ideas. Who has given them these faculties? Who has made the grass of the fields to grow, and the earth to revolve about the sun?

Antiquity

At some time in every town Adam Adams and his wife try to get at the head of the procession by saying, "Our ancestors were here first." But since nobody knows for sure whether they were or not, proof must be found; their honor is at stake. Then an old broken chamber pot is dug up, marked with the maker's initial A, and Adam Adams declares that it was part of his great-great grandmother's teapot. Just so Caesar must have proved that he was descended from Venus. History abounds in such records, particularly in early antiquity.

Scholars in Armenia were wont to demonstrate that the earthly paradise was in their country. Learned Swedes demonstrated that it was in the vicinity of Lake Wenner, which they said still bore traces of it. Spaniards placed it in Castille. And a Scotchman proved that the garden of Eden was in Edinburgh — witness the survival of the name.

Appearances

ARE all appearances deceptive? Have our senses been given us only to trick us? Is everything error? Do we live in a dream? We see the sun still setting when it is below the horizon. A square tower seems to be round. A straight stick in water seems to be bent. You see your face in a mirror; the image appears to be behind the glass when it is neither behind nor before it. The glass itself, seemingly so smooth and even, is made up of tiny projections and pits. The finest and fairest skin is a bristling net of minute hairs. What is large to us is small to an elephant; what is small may be a whole world to an insect.

Nothing is either as it appears to be, or where we think it is. Philosophers, weary of being deceived, have in their petulance declared that nothing exists but what is in our mind. They might have gone all the way and concluded that, the nature of the mind being as elusive as that of matter, there is nothing real either in matter or mind. Perhaps it is in this despair of ever knowing anything that certain Chinese philosophers say that nothing is the beginning and end of all things.

You do not see the net of hairs of the white and delicate skin you idolize. Organisms a thousand times less than a mite perceive what escapes your vision; they lodge, feed, and travel about on it as in an extensive country; those on a right arm are ignorant that creatures of their own species exist on a left. If you were so unfortunate as to see what they see, this charming skin would transfix you with horror.

All is in due proportion. The laws of optics, which show you an object where it is not, make the sun appear two feet in diameter when it is a million times larger than the earth, a size impossible for your eye to encompass. Our senses assist much more than they deceive us.

Motion, time, hardness, softness, size, distance, appearances, all are relative. And Who has created the delicate adjustments of relativities?

Beauty

PLATO is quoted on love, so why not on beauty, since beauty engenders love? It is instructive to know what a Greek wrote of beauty more than two thousand years ago:

"The man initiated into the sacred mysteries, seeing a beautiful face together with a divine form, feels emotion surge within him, as well as a sort of worshipping fear. This is godhead. . . . Beauty enters into his soul through his eyes; the wings of his soul melt; they lose the stiffness of their fibre and liquefy; renewed they sprout, as it were, from every part of the soul (which once had wings) . . . ."

I concede the fineness of this passage of the divine Plato, but it fails to give us a very clear idea of the nature of beauty.

To a toad what is beauty? A female with two lovely pop-eyes, a wide mouth, yellow belly, and green spotted back. To a Negro of Guinea what is beauty? A black oily skin, blubber lips, a flat nose. To the devil? Horns, claws, and a tail. To the philosophers? Ask them and they reply in jargon. One night I sat next to a philosopher at a play. "How beautiful it is!" he exclaimed. "In what way?" I inquired. "It has," he replied, "achieved its end."

The next day I met the philosopher after he had taken some effective medicine. "It has achieved its end," I remarked. "It must be very beautiful."

After some discussion he concluded that beauty is relative, just as what may be decent in Japan is indecent in Rome, or what may be fashionable in Paris is not so in Peking. That saved him the trouble of composing a long dissertation on beauty.

Bees

BEES are superior to the human race in this: they produce from themselves substances that are useful, while of all our secretions none is good for anything—indeed, they all render us disagreeable.

Swarms which leave a hive are milder than our sons when they leave college. The young bees then sting no one, save rarely in an extraordinary case. They allow themselves to be carried quietly on the bare hand to the new hive awaiting them. But when they are settled in their new home they become possessive, like us, and make war. I have seen bees laboring peaceably among the flowers in a meadow for months, but when mowers came they rushed furiously from their hive to drive away those who were stealing their property.

Books

So you think nothing of books, you who strive for great things, or pleasure, or prefer indolence. Remember that the whole world, save only the savage parts, is under the sway of books. Northern Africa, to the borders of Ethiopia and Nigritia, obeys the Koran, having given up the Gospels. China is ruled by the books of Confucius, and a great part of India by the Vedas. Persia was governed for ages by the books of one of the Zoroasters.

If you get into a lawsuit or criminal trial, your property, your honor, and perhaps your life depend on the interpretation of books you have never read. There are mediocre books to be sure; but among both books and men a small number play a large part, and the rest belong to the undistinguished.

Who lead their fellow men in all civilized countries? Those who can read and write. You may not be acquainted with Hippocrates, Boerhaave, or Sydenham, yet you place your body in the hands of those who have read them. And you place your soul in the care of those who are paid to read the Scriptures, though only a handful may have read them through with attention.

There are countries where thought is held to be a mere article of commerce, valued at so much a sheet. If the bookseller wants a license for his merchandise, whether he be selling Rabelais or the Christian Fathers, he must get it from the authorities, but need not be responsible for what his books contain. And there are countries where the liberty of expressing yourself in books is one of the most inviolable prerogatives. There you may print whatever you please, even on pain of being a bore, or of having a surfeit of your natural right.

Before the invaluable invention of printing, books were scarcer and more costly than jewels. Even in Russia in the year 1700 you would have found few books save missals and Bibles, and those were in the hands of clergymen groggy with vodka.

But now the trouble is that we have too many books. Readers need not complain, however; they are not forced to read them—nor are authors compelled to write them. Yet with all this abundance how few people read! If only more would take to books, we should see less of the misinformation that is rife among us.

Books know no law of moderate increase, because books are made from books. A new history is manufactured from existing volumes. Dictionaries are made from dictionaries. Almost all geographies are made from geographies. The same race of bookworms that burrowed through the parents is now tunneling through the children.

It is sometimes very dangerous to make a book. There is hardly a single philosophical or theological book in which heresies and impieties may not be found by misinterpreting, or adding to or subtracting from the sense. Thus Theodore of Mopsuestes ventured to call the Song of Songs "a collection of impurities"; Grotius pulled it apart and said it was nasty; Chatillon spoke of it as "a scandalous production."

Perhaps it will hardly be believed that Dr. Tamponet maintained, "I could set out to find a number of heresies in the Lord's Prayer, which we know to have come from Divine lips, if it had only recently been published by a Jesuit. I should proceed thus: 'Our Father, which art in heaven,' —a proposition tending toward heresy, since God is everywhere; — 'Thy kingdom come, Thy will be done on earth as it is in heaven' — another proposition tainted with heresy, for again and again Scriptures say that God reigns eternally; moreover, it is rash to ask that His will be done, since nothing is or can be done but by the will of God; — 'give us this day our daily bread' — a proposition directly contrary to what Jesus Christ uttered, 'Take no thought, saying what shall we eat, or what shall we drink . . . for after all these things do the Gentiles seek . . . but seek ye first the kingdom of God'; — 'forgive us our debts as we forgive our debtors' — a rash proposition which compares man to God, destroys gratuitous predestination, and assumes that God is bound to do to us as we do to others; besides, no convent in Europe ever remitted to its farmers a single penny;—'lead us not into temptation,'—a proposition scandalous and manifestly heretical, for

there is no tempter but the devil. You see, then,"
said Dr. Tamponet, "that there is nothing, be it
ever so venerable, but that may be given a twist
for the worse."

If you publish a book, a parish curate accuses
you of heresy, a college sophomore denounces

you, an illiterate condemns you, the public derides you, your publisher renounces you, and your wine dealer cuts off your credit. I always add to my prayers, "Deliver me, O Lord, from the itch of bookmaking." You who, like myself, spot black and white and make clean paper dirty, take heed of these verses which I read somewhere, and which should have given us pause:

> This miscellaneous rubbish once was flax,
> Till made soft linen by the honest weaver;
> But when at length it dropped from people's backs,
> 'Twas turned to paper, and became receiver
> Of all that fifty motley brains could fashion;
> So now 'tis burned without the least compassion;
> It now, like glory, terminates in smoke;
> Thus all our toils are nothing but a joke—
> All ends in smoke; each nothing that we follow
> Tells of the nothing that must all things swallow.

Caesar

NOT as the lover of so many women and the beloved of so many men, not as the conqueror of Pompey and the Scipios, not as the orator who decimated Cato, not as the robber of the public treasury who used Roman money to subjugate Romans, nor as the clement victor, the scholar who reformed the calendar, the tyrant and father of his country, assassinated by his friends and illegitimate son, shall Caesar here be treated. I'll speak of him only as I see him, I, a descendant from the poor barbarians whom he subjugated.

You cannot pass through a town in France, Spain, on the banks of the Rhine, or on the English coast opposite Calais, where people do not boast that Caesar slept there. Some of the towns-folk of Dover are persuaded that Caesar built their castle; and there are Parisians who believe that the Chatelet is one of his works. Many a French squire can show you his dovecote, a turret built, of course, by Caesar. Each province disputes with its neighbor the honor of having been the first to which Caesar applied the lash; it was not by this road but by that, that he came to cut our throats, rape our wives and daughters, impose—through interpreters—his laws on us, and take what little money we had.

An Italian historian, passing through Vannes in Brittany, was surprised to hear the local antiquarians speak of Caesar as if he had been there only the day before. "You have some monument of his?" he asked. "Oh, yes," they replied. "We can show you where he had our entire senate of the province, six hundred of them, hung. Some beams were excavated there — the ignorant believed them to be the foundation of a bridge—but we have papers to prove that they were gallows. What other town in Gaul can boast so much? We are the one mentioned in the *Commentaries,* who 'are fickle and prefer liberty to slavery.' "

In India they have but vague knowledge of the robber (name, Alexander) who descended upon them, and scarcely ever speak of him; the Indians are wiser than we.

Cannibals

IN 1725 four savages were brought from the Mississippi to Fontainebleau. I had the honor of conversing with them. Among them was a young woman whom I asked if she had eaten men. "Of course," she answered with great simplicity. I appeared to be a little scandalized, whereupon she continued, "Is it not better to eat one's dead enemy than to leave him to be devoured by wild beasts? Surely victors deserve the spoils. We kill our neighbors in fights or skirmishes, and for the most trifling reasons, then leave them to the crows and worms. In killing is the horror and the crime; what does it matter when a man is dead whether he be eaten by a soldier or by a vulture?"

Cato
(AND SUICIDE)

IT was, I believe, because of Cato's equipoise that he retained to the last a love for his country and her laws, choosing to perish with her rather than to bow to a tyrant.

He died as he had lived, incapable of being swayed, incapable of surrender.

Suicide is forbidden us, but it was not illegal to Cato, to Brutus, to Cassius, to the sublime Arria, to the Emperor Otho, to Mark Anthony, and to those other true Romans who preferred death at their own hand to a life which they saw as ignominious.

We kill ourselves, however, but only when we have lost our money or when — in an excess of foolish passion — it is for an unworthy object. I have known women who killed themselves for the most stupid men imaginable. Sometimes, too, we kill ourselves when we are in bad health, an act of weakness. Boredom with existence, weariness with ourselves, is another cause of suicide. The remedy for this is a little exercise, music, hunting, the theatre, or an agreeable woman. The man who, in a fit of melancholy, kills himself today would have wished to live had he waited a week.

We are not informed about it, but it is unlikely that the inhabitants of Great Britain killed themselves in the time of Caesar so deliberately as they do now when they have the vapors. On the other hand the Romans, who never had the vapors, did not hesitate to put themselves to death. They reasoned, they were philosophers; the people of Britain were not. Now the English are philosophers and the ancient Romans are no more. The Englishman quits this life proudly and disdainfully when it is his whim. The Roman must have had an *indulgentia in articulo mortis;* he could neither live nor die.

William Temple says that a man should depart when he no longer takes any pleasure in remaining. So died Atticus. Young women who hang and drown themselves for love should be cautioned to reconsider, for changes in love are at least as frequent as in other affairs.

To save yourself from the desire of self-destruction always have something to do. Creech, the commentator on Lucretius, made notes on his manuscript, "N.B. Don't forget: hang myself when finished." He heeded the notes in order to have the pleasure of ending as had his author. Had he been working on a commentary upon Ovid he would have lived longer.

Why are there fewer suicides in the country than in town? Because on the land only the body grows tired; on the pavements it is the mind. The laborer has no time to be melancholy. None kill themselves but the idle, those who seem, to the worker, such happy people.

Celibacy

THE first Christians did not consider celibacy a virtue. Nearly all the apostles and disciples were married. St. Paul wrote to Titus, "Choose for a priest him who is the husband of one wife, having believing children, and not under accusation of dissoluteness." The proceedings of the Council of Nice on the subject of married priests deserve attention. Some bishops proposed that priests thenceforward put away their wives, but St. Paphnucius the Martyr, bishop of Thebes in Egypt, strenuously opposed it, observing that marriage was chastity; and the Council adopted his opinion.

After that time celibacy was recommended the clergy without being commanded. St. Jerome, a devout recluse, was of all the fathers highest in his eulogiums of celibacy in priests, yet he resolutely supported the cause of Carterius, a Spanish bishop who had been married twice. "Were I to enumerate," said he, "all the bishops who have entered into second nuptials, I should name as many as were present at the Council of Rimini."

At length, after several councils on the subject of celibacy had been held without effect, Pope Gregory excommunicated all married priests, either to add respectability to the Church by the greater rigor of its discipline, or to attach more closely to Rome the bishops and priests of other countries, who would thus have no other family than the Church.

Climate

THE sun and atmosphere certainly have their effect on everything in nature from man to mushrooms. The ingenious Fontenelle remarked, "One would think that the torrid and frigid zones are not well suited to the development of the sciences." Chardin goes still further, saying, "The temperature of warm regions enervates the mind as well as the body, and dissipates that fire which makes the imagination combust into invention. In such a climate men are incapable of long study and the intense application which are necessary for first-rate production in the arts and sciences." And Boindin asserts that climate determines both political and religious forms.

But if climate is so strong an influencing factor, why is it that the Emperor Julian, in his *Misopogon*, comments on the pleasing gravity of character and severity of manners of the ancient Parisians, while the Parisians of today, without the slightest change of climate, are playful as children, smiling, singing, and lampooning their masters? In his letters Cicero was not above joking about the English; he asked his brother Quintus whether, on his expedition to Britain, he had found any notable philosophers among them. He little suspected that the island would one day produce scientists whose ideas he could not have understood. Yet the climate has not changed; the London sky is as overcast now as it was then.

But everything is changed, both bodies and minds, by the passage of time. Perhaps the Americans will in some future period cross the ocean to instruct Europeans in the arts. Climate has

27

some influence, government much more, and the combination of religion and government most of all.

Character

From the Greek word signifying *impression, engraving*—it is what nature has engraved in us.

CAN we change our character? Yes, if we change our body. A man born turbulent, violent, and stubborn, may, through falling into an apoplexy in his old age, become like a quiet, weak, tractable child. His body is no longer the same. But so long as his nerves, blood, and marrow remain unaltered, his disposition will change no more than the instinct of a wolf or polecat.

Religion and morality curb the strength of the disposition, but cannot destroy it. The drunkard in a cloister, limited to a glass of cider a meal, will never get drunk but will always be fond of drink. Age weakens the character; it is an old tree, producing only a few puny fruits — but always the same, acorns or apples. If we could change our character we could become the master of nature. We perfect, we ameliorate, we conceal what nature has placed in us, but we can place nothing

28

there ourselves. One passion devours the rest, but is that a triumph? Are we not all like the old general of ninety who, having found some young officers behaving in a rather disorderly manner with some young women, said to them in anger, "Gentlemen, is this the example that I set you?"

Common Sense

THERE is sometimes in ordinary expressions a figure that emerges from deep in the heart of all men. *Sensus communis* signified among the Romans not only common sense, but also humanity and sensibility. We are not the equal of the Romans; with us the expression conveys not half so much. It signifies only good sense—plain, forthright reasoning—a notion of what ordinary things are, something between dullness and keenness of intellect. To say, "he has no common sense," is a gross insult; while "he has common sense" is an affront also: it would imply being not quite stupid, but lacking in brains. But what is the meaning of common sense, if it be not sense? When this term originated, men supposed that nothing entered the mind save by the senses; otherwise would they have used the word sense to signify perception?

Sometimes it is said that common sense is rare. What does this mean? That, in many, dawning reason is stopped by prejudice; that one who judges reasonably in one instance will be badly mistaken in another. The Arab who may have been a good mathematician, a learned chemist, and an exact astronomer, nevertheless believed that Mohamet put half the moon into his sleeve. His head being a muddle of ideas about this sleeve which he could not perceive, he feared to disentangle them, and thus relinquished common sense.

Crime

A ROMAN in Egypt happened unfortunately to kill a sacred cat, and the infuriated people punished the sacrilege by tearing him to pieces. If this Roman had been taken before a tribunal, and the judges had been wise, they would have condemned him to ask pardon of the Egyptians and the cats, and to pay a heavy fine, either in money or in mice. They would have told him to respect the peccadillos of the people if he had not the power to correct them.

We think nothing of a statue in the house. Yet if when Octavius, surnamed Augustus, was absolute master, a Roman had harbored a statue of Brutus in his house, he would have been punished as seditious. Or if an Englishman, having nothing better to do, had gone to Rome and there met Prince Charles Edward in the house of a cardinal, and had been pleased with him and returned home and drunk his health in a tavern, he would immediately have been accused of high treason. If he should have conspired to place him on the throne, then he would have been guilty toward the nation. But I cannot see that the most rigid justice of Parliament could have required more of him than to drink four cups to the health of the house of Hanover, should he have drunk two to the house of Stuart.

Democracy

As a rule no comparison can be made between the crimes of the great, who are always ambitious, and those of the people, who never desire, and who never can desire, anything but liberty and equality. While liberty and equality do not necessarily lead to calumny, rapine, assassination, poisoning, and devastation of neighboring lands, the towering ambition and thirst for power of the great precipitate them into every species of crime, no matter what the place or period.

The great vice of democracy is certainly not tyranny and cruelty. There have been republicans in mountainous regions who were wild and ferocious, but they were made so not by the spirit of republicanism but by nature. The basic vice of a civilized republic is symbolized in the Turkish fable of the dragon with many heads and the dragon with many tails. The many heads may prove aggressive, but the tails follow the one head when it wants to devour everything.

Democracy seems to suit only a very small country, and that only when fortunately situated. Small as it may be, it will have many faults, because it will be composed of men. Discord will prevail in it, but there will be no St. Bartholomew there, no Irish massacre, no Inquisition.

Dictionary

HERE I shall treat of only that new species of historical dictionary which contains a collection of lies and satires in alphabetical order, such as the *Historical, Literary, and Critical Dictionary,* containing a summary of the lives of celebrated men of all sorts, printed in 1758 in six volumes, octavo, without the name of an author. In dictionaries like this, which are full of party prejudice, one rarely finds what one wants to look up, and often what one does not. The gentlemanly writer of the articles will, for instance, exhibit every bad verse that has ever been composed on the French Academy, together with anecdotes as silly as they are false, evidently out of pure zeal for religion.

He will assert, moreover, that the Abbé Gedoyn slept with the celebrated Ninon de l'Enclos on her eightieth birthday night; the story is an old one: it is told of the Abbé Châteauneuf and Ninon when she was sixty. In early life, as it happens, I saw a great deal of the Abbé Gedoyn and Mlle. de l'Enclos. I can vouch for it that at the age of eighty her face bore the most hideous marks of old age, that her body was racked with all the infirmities of the octogenarian, and that her mind was given to an austere philosophy.

Divorce

THE Justinian code, which we have adopted in several points, authorizes divorce; but the canonical law, which the Catholics hold before it, gives divorce no sanction.

Divorce is probably coeval with marriage. Naturally, marriage is a few weeks more ancient, I believe; men quarrelled with their wives after five days, beat them after a month, and separated from them after six weeks.

Justinian was a Christian and even a theologian. How is it, then, that the Church derogates from his laws? As it alone took cognizance of marriage, so it alone judged of divorces. No prince effected a divorce and married a second wife without previously obtaining the consent of the pope. Henry VIII of England did not marry without his consent, until after having a long time solicited in vain his divorce in Rome. This custom, established in ignorant times, is perpetuated in enlightened ones. All abuse is self-eternalizing.

Dog

NATURE, it seems, has given the dog to man for his defense and pleasure. Of all animals it is the most faithful; it is man's best possible friend. Why then has the word dog become an injurious term? We say when we are tender, my sparrow, my dove, my chicken; we even say my kitten, though this animal is notoriously treacherous. But when we are angry we call people dogs! The Turks, when not even angry, speak with horror and contempt of the Christian dogs. The English, when they see a man who looks as if he had been born on the banks of the Seine or the Loire, customarily call him a French dog — a rhetorical sally neither just to the dog nor polite to the man. Of course sensitive Homer makes the divine Achilles tell the divine Agamemnon that he is impudent as a dog, a classical justification for the English man in the street.

In spite of all, the dog is honored by permanent residence in the heavens, in the dog star. And we think of him in the dog days.

FERNALD LIBRARY
COLBY JUNIOR COLLEGE
NEW LONDON, NEW HAMPSHIRE

I just notice with regret that I have omitted an article on cats; but perhaps I can here make amends by referring to a little of their history. While there are no cats in the heavens, as there are goats, crabs, bulls, rams, eagles, lions, fishes, rabbits, and dogs, the cat by way of recompense has been held sacred, and has been revered, adored, sainted in many places, and considered altogether divine by no small number of women.

Elegance

ACCORDING to certain authors, this word comes from *electus,* chosen; it seems that its etymology can come from no other Latin word, as all that is choice is elegant. Elegance is the result of regularity and grace.

The word is often employed in speaking of painting and sculpture. *Elegans signum* is opposed to *signum rigens* — a proportionate figure, the rounded form of which is softly modeled, to a harsh and rudely-finished figure.

The severity of the ancient Romans gave a derogatory sense to the word *elegantia.* They regarded elegance in any form as affectation and foppishness, unworthy of the gravity of a pristine age. They called an elegant what we should call a *petit-maitre* or beau. But in the time of Cicero, when manners achieved great refinement, *elegans* was always deemed laudatory.

Among the French as among the ancient Romans the term is confined to sculpture, painting, eloquence, and especially poetry; it is not at all the same in meaning as graceful.

The word graceful applies to a countenance or

32328

body; we do not say an elegant face as we say an elegant sweep. Grace springs from movement, in mind or in features.

The elegance of a discourse does not lie in its eloquence; it is inherent. It is not in the flow and cadence, but in the clarity of thought and choice of expression. A discourse may be elegant without being good, for elegance is just a sort of selectivity, but a discourse cannot be really good

without being elegant. To poetry elegance is even more necessary than eloquence, because it is of the stuff that poetry is made. An orator may persuade and convince without elegance, but a poet cannot; elegance is one of the virtues of Virgil. Horace in his satires and epistles is much less elegant, and in that degree he is less a poet.

Poetry and oratory should never appear to have a forced elegance. The poet has a harder time in this than the orator, for he deals in the most delicate choice of word music. Sometimes he must even sacrifice his thought somewhat to his diction, a constraint the orator need never feel. And if elegance postulates ease, all that is easy and natural is not therefore elegant.

Drama may seldom be said to be elegantly written. Naturalistic dialogue precludes it. And elegance is even inconsistent with comedy. A thing elegantly said would not be laughed at. Conversely, elegance cannot be thought of in connection with the sublime. To call the Jupiter Olympus of Phidias elegant would be to belittle it. On the other hand there would be good reason to speak of the elegance of the Venus of Praxiteles.

Eloquence

ELOQUENCE came before the rules of rhetoric, as languages come before grammar.

Nature renders men eloquent under the influence of great interests or passions. An excited person sees things with a special eye. He can compare by metaphor. Without study he can make everything lively so that his listeners may partake of his enthusiasm. To him the heart burns, courage is kindled, the eyes sparkle; the mind is oppressed, divided, or exhausted; blood freezes, the head turns topsy-turvy; we are inflated with pride and intoxicated with vengeance. Nature is revealed by strong images, which enter the language as common expressions.

Nature inspires spontaneous sallies. When a captain of the caliphs saw his men running away from the battlefield he cried, "Where are you going? Your enemy is not there!" Or an English sailor in the war against Spain of 1740 recounted, "The Spaniards had mutilated me and were going to kill me. I gave my soul to God and my vengeance to my country!"

Greece, it may be remarked, was the only ancient land in which the laws of eloquence were known, because it was the only one in which true eloquence existed. The grosser art was known to all men; but to rouse the minds of a whole cultivated nation, to please, convince, and move at the same time, belonged only to the Greeks. The orientals were then slaves for the most part; it is a servile trait to exaggerate everything; thus Asiatic eloquence was overblown. In the time of Aristotle the west was barbarous. But true eloquence began to emerge in the time of the Gracchi. Marc Anthony, Hortensius, Curion, Caesar, and many others were eloquent. This eloquence perished with the republic, as it had in Athens. Inspired eloquence, it is said, belongs only to liberty. It consists in telling bold truths and giving strong reasons and figures.

When truth is disliked and reason is feared, a well-turned compliment succeeds better than inspired eloquence.

Great eloquence scarcely exists at the bar in

37

France, because it does not lead to honors, as it did in Athens and Rome and does in London. Nor has it the public interest for its object. It is saved for funeral orations, which border a little upon—poetry.

May a historian be eloquent? His art consists in arranging an account of events in some well-written exposition, in being sometimes lively and circumstantial, sometimes sonorous, in being strong and true so far as go his pictures of background and chief figures. But the eloquence of Demosthenes would ill fit Thucydides. A studied harangue put into the mouth of a hero who never pronounced it would be nothing to a history but a splendid defect.

Much more might be said upon the subject, but books on eloquence have already said too much, and in an enlightened age genius, aided by examples on every side, knows more than could be taught by all the masters.

Enchantment

THE derivation of the word enchantment (*incantatio*) is said to be from the Greek by way of the Chaldean, meaning "song that has power to move." Thus it was believed that Orpheus made stones and trees dance. If this ballet was so simple, a city might be built with a violin or razed with a ram's horn.

The charming of snakes, like the flocking together of domestic animals at the farmer's call, is not done by magic. Reptiles are really timid. The first thing a reptile does upon seeing a man, at least in Europe, is to scuttle for cover. So a man pursues everything that runs from him, and runs from everything that pursues him, except when he is armed or knows that he is being watched.

Serpents, far from being voracious, pass long periods without eating at all; and when they do eat, they only destroy a field mouse or a few insects. There were, of course, the serpents that came all the way from Tenedos hell-bent for eating Laocoon and his two grown twenty-year-old sons, in the sight of the whole Trojan army. This was a notable exception, fit to transmit to posterity in hexameter verses, and in a statue where the strapping lads are shown frightened out of several years' growth. All this happened, naturally, when cities that had been built by the gods were taken by armies hidden in a wooden horse, when rivers on occasion flowed backwards, water was changed to blood, and both the sun and moon had a way of standing still upon the slightest provocation.

There was undoubtedly enchantment in those days.

Enchantments to kindle love were hawked by the Jews in ancient Rome and Alexandria, and are still sold in parts of Asia. You can read in Apuleius how he was accused by a Christian whose daughter he had married of having bewitched her by philtres. It was claimed that these were made of fish, and Venus having been born of the sea, fish were supposed to have a great amorous influence. Apuleius was accused of having used, specifically, periwinkles, lobster patties, female sea-urchins, spiced oysters, and squid, celebrated for its fertility.

What he really used to enchant the Christian's daughter was neither music nor love-potion, as he explained. He admitted that the girl had called him a magician. "But," said he, "if she had called me a consul that wouldn't have made me one."

Youth and health are the greatest philtres. When some of our debilitated rakes took chocolate because of the reputation it enjoyed among them, they could take twenty cups without becoming any more winning. *Ut amoris amabilis esto,* says Ovid: "Wouldst thou be loved, be amiable."

English Drama

I HAVE been looking through a new edition of Shakespeare made by one Samuel Johnson. He remarks that foreigners are obtuse when they are surprised to find a comic Roman senator or a drunken king on the stage in the plays of the great Shakespeare. I do not wish to hint that this Mr. Johnson is a sorry jester or too fond of his drink, but I do find it rather extraordinary that he includes slapstick and inebriety among the beauties of tragedy. His reasons are no less curious. He says that the dramatist disdains accidental distinctions—like the painter who, having got a figure done, pays little further attention to its drapery. The comparison would have been better had he spoken of a painter of heroic figures who introduced ridiculous grotesques among them, for instance Alexander the Great at the battle of Arbela seated on an ass, or Darius' wife carousing at an inn.

The most singular point is that Shakespeare is really a genius. The Italian, French, and other men of letters who have not spent some time in

his country take him only for a clown, a comic
inferior to Harlequin, the most contemptible
jack-a-pudding that ever played to the gallery.
Yet it is this man who can exalt the imagination
and stir the heart to its depths. It is Truth, it is
Nature herself, speaking out in her own language
without artificiality. This sublimity seems not
of the author's seeking.

The famous Addison knew, however, how to
guide genius with taste. He had correct style, dis-
creet invention, elegance, and strong simplicity
in his prose and verse. A friend of propriety and
order, he wrote tragedy with dignity; it is thus
that his *Cato* is composed.

Equality

THIS fact is perfectly clear. Men, in the functions
common to all of them, are equal. They are equal
in their mechanism and in the ability to use their
senses. The emperor of China, the great mogul,
or the Turkish pasha could never say to the low-
est of his subjects, "I forbid you to digest your
food, discharge the waste, or think." Animals of
every species are on this plane of equality with
each other. If a bull, while paying his attentions
to a cow, is driven away by the horns of another
bull stronger than himself, he goes to seek another
cow in another meadow, and lives in freedom. A
defeated cock finds consolation in another hen-
roost. Not so with men. A petty vizier may banish
a bostangi to Lemnos; the pasha banishes the
vizier to Rhodes; janissaries imprison the pasha
and elect another who in turn banishes the worthy
faithful when and where he pleases, while they

feel inexpressibly grateful to him for such a merciful display of his authority.

If the earth were all that it should be, if men could find easy and certain subsistence everywhere, together with a pleasant climate, obviously it would be impossible for one man to subjugate another. Should the globe be covered with wholesome fruits, and the air be so salubrious that we had no disease or premature death, man would require no more lodging than does the deer or roebuck, and Genghis Khans and Tamerlanes would have no other followers than their own families, who would be worthy persons, willing to serve them affectionately in their old age.

In that state of nature enjoyed by wild creatures, men would be as happy as they. Subservience would be ridiculous. What servants would be necessary when no service would be required?

If it should occur to someone with a talent for the tyrannical and an itching fist, to subjugate his less powerful neighbor, he would fail in his project. The victims would be on the Danube before the aggressor had completed preparations on the Volga.

All men would necessarily be equal if they had no wants. It is man's misery that makes him an underdog; inequality is not the real grievance, but dependence. It matters little if one man be called his highness and another his holiness so long as none is called his lordship.

Say that one large family lives on a good piece of land and two small ones on poor land nearby. In order to live the poor families must serve the rich one, or attempt to destroy it. Now suppose that one poor family offers its services to the rich one for bread, and the other attacks it and is worsted. The first become servitors, the second slaves.

In this melancholy world it is impossible for men living in society not to become divided into the rich who command and the poor who obey. You may protest that you have two hands and feel just like the other fellow, and maybe a little more pride; that you have a mind as poor, slight, and muddled as his, and that you therefore want your fair share of land. You may point out that there are fifty billion acres of good land, and a thousand million two-footed, featherless inhabitants of them, and demand your fifty. But wherever you ask them you will be told, get them from the Kaffirs or Hottentots or Samoyeds; there's no room for you here. If you want food and lodging here, you'll be told to work for somebody to get them; serve or amuse and you'll be paid; if you won't, you'll have to beg, and that will be highly degrading to your lofty nature, and keep you from associating with kings, or even village curates, with whom you claim equality.

All the poor are not unhappy. Most of the poor are born that way; they have their work to keep them from feeling their situation too keenly. When they do become aware of it, there is a war, and the war is settled sooner or later by their resubjugation. For the masters have capital, and capital commands all within a state. But in a war between states, the one with the best iron may come out the winner over the one with more gold.

Every man is born with a will for power, wealth, and pleasure, and a way that is indolent. Every man consequently covets the goods, wife, or daughter of another; he wants to command

and see others move at his bidding; and he wants to be idle, or to do nothing that is not perfectly agreeable. It is clear that men, having such amiable dispositions, can no more be equal than can a couple of preachers or teachers of divinity not be jealous of each other.

Constituted as it is, the human race cannot exist without vast numbers of workers who have no property at all, for certainly a man in easy circumstances will not leave his own land to cultivate yours; and if you want a pair of shoes you'll not get a lawyer to make them for you. Equality is, then, both the most natural and the most impossible of things for men.

Fiction

SUPPOSING that it brings home truth, what is wrong with fiction? Don't you like the story of the sultan who, disbelieving that a moment could be long, disputed with his dervish on the nature of duration? The latter, to convince him, asked him to put his head into a basin for a moment. Straightway the sultan found himself in a terrible desert; he had to live by the sweat of his brow; he married and had children who grew up to torment him; after five and twenty years he found his way back to his own country and palace, lifted his head, and saw the basin and dervish before him.

As for fiction which shows nothing and gets nowhere, what is it but untruth? Or fiction which rambles on from one unrelated situation to another, is it any better than a meaningless dream?

It may be pointed out that certain classic tales

are incoherent, without ingenuity, and even absurd. If they are still admired it is because of their fine details rather than their general framework. I won't belabor the point, but if you want to be given bad reviews and afterwards be condemned to oblivion, take one of those tales for your model.

Filial Respect

"JUST between you and me, sir, my father is a drunkard. He begot me by accident and doesn't care a hoot for me. My mother is no better than she should be. If it hadn't been for my nurse, who took a liking to me and brought me up as her own son, I couldn't have been alive today. Must I honor my father and mother?"

"Well—honor your nurse; and nod politely to your father and mother if you meet them."

"One word more, sir. If my father had been Abraham and I Isaac, and he had said, 'My son, you are grown tall and strong; carry these faggots to the top of the hill; I'll burn you with them after I've cut off your head, as God ordered me to when He came to see me this morning,' what should I have done?"

"What *would* you have done?"

"I'd have asked him to produce a written order. And I'd have said, 'Father, you are among strangers. Think of yourself; take due precaution. Others have been broken on the wheel for matters less than this when they were without a proper permit signed in God's handwriting. If you haven't got one I'll have to go to Pharoah or the King of Gerar — both were fond of Mother, you know — and they'll take my part. Cut my

45

brother Ishmael's throat if you like, but not mine, thanks.' "

"Well reasoned. I admire you for the respect you would have shown Abraham, and for not being tempted to light into him. Now tell me, if you had been Cram, whose father Clothaire the Frankish king had him burned in a barn, or Don Carlos, son of that old fox Philip II, or poor Alexis, son of Czar Peter—"

"Please, sir, no more or I shall begin to like even my own parents."

Finesse

FINENESS, or finesse, figuratively applies to conduct, speech, and emanations of the mind. Finesse in conduct, as in the arts, always implies something delicate or subtle; it may exist without art, but rarely without a little deception. It is to be found in politics, but is reproved by society.

Finesse is not exactly subtlety; we draw a person into a snare with finesse; he escapes from it with subtlety. We act with finesse, but we retract with subtlety. Distrust is inspired by too much finesse, yet we frequently deceive ourselves in suspecting it.

Finesse in wit consists of clouding a thought so that it may be all the more clearly perceived. It poses a sort of transparent enigma. A chancellor once offered his protection to Parliament. The speaker, turning toward the assembly, said, "Gentlemen, thank the chancellor. He has given us more than we have asked." A witty reproof.

In conversation and writing finesse differs from delicacy. It may be applied to piquant and agreeable things, to praise and blame, and even to indecencies, over which a veil is drawn so that we may see without being called upon to blush. The boldest statements may be made with finesse.

Franchise

THE word always conveys the idea of liberty; it is derived from the Franks, who were always free. It is so ancient that when the Cid besieged and took Toledo in the eleventh century, franchies or franchises were given to all the French who went on the expedition and settled in Toledo. All walled cities had franchises, liberties, and privileges, even in the greatest period of feudal anarchy. In all countries with states and assemblies, the sovereign swore on his accession to guard their liberties.

Franchise signifies liberty of speech, or of getting counsel, or of legal right, but there is a great difference between free speech and frank speech.

To a superior, free speech that is bold and frank is unwarranted. Speech too free becomes audacious, too frank becomes too open-hearted.

Fraud

THE fakir Bambabef one day encountered a disciple of Confutzee (whom we call Confucius); the disciple was named Wang. Bambabef argued that people need to be deceived but Wang maintained that they should never have the wool pulled over their eyes. This is what they said:

BAMBABEF. The example of the Supreme Being should be followed; He never shows us things as they are. He makes us see the sun as a disc only a couple of feet in diameter, though it is a million times larger than the earth; He makes us see the moon and stars as objects on the same blue plane, whereas they are at greatly varying distances. In short, He surrounds us with error, to reach our comprehension.

WANG. This is not error; we only perceive it in error, needing the proper instruments to see it aright.

BAMBABEF. At least you must acknowledge this. A physician may deceive a child for its own good, saying he is giving it sugar when he gives it rhubarb.

WANG. I have never deceived my two sons. When they were sick I told them, "Take this nasty medicine; you'll need courage to swallow it, but something pleasant wouldn't help you." I never let their nurse or tutor scare them with ghosts, goblins, and witches. Thereby I have made them courageous and wise.

BAMBABEF. The majority of people are not so fortunate as your sons.

WANG. People are all much the same at birth. They should not be warped by education.

BAMBABEF. We mislead them, I'll admit, but it is for their benefit. We tell them that if they do not buy our holy talismans, or if they do not give us money to expiate their sins, they will become beasts of burden, dogs, or lizards in the next life. That frightens them into being good.

WANG. But you are perverting them! Surely there are some who can see that they won't become dogs and lizards; they know that you are talking nonsense, and think that there is no religion at all because the one you show them is so ridiculous. You are responsible for the vices into which they plunge.

BAMBABEF. Not at all. We teach only virtue.

WANG. You'd be stoned if you taught vice. Men are so constituted that they like vice without wanting it taught them. But precepts of morality should not be intermixed with absurd fables. These impostures, which you might well do without, weaken the morality you preach.

BAMBABEF. Then you think that truth can be shown the people without the aid of fables?

WANG. We do not need to teach our literate classes by indirection, and why should we have to teach others so?

BAMBABEF. There must be white bread for the master and brown for the servant.

WANG. I own that all men do not need to be taught the same skills, but there are things that all should know. They should be just, and the surest way of inculcating justice is to inspire them by a religion without superstition.

BAMBABEF. That's impractical. If some, as you say, won't take fables, others won't take the truth. They'll demand proofs—some sort of a miracle to show that you have divine backing. Then where are you?

WANG. You argue that men will spurn ideas that are honest, plausible, and useful just because they reject those which are dishonest, absurd, and useless. There is no need of a miracle to believe in a just God, who reads the heart of man. This is an idea too natural and necessary to reject. We have whole towns with scarcely any other tenet, and in them I have seen abundant virtue.

Government

THERE must be some exquisite pleasure in governing, to judge from the numbers who are eager to be concerned in it. We have more books on government than governors in the world. I don't want to set myself up as an instructor to kings and their ministers, valets, confessors, and treasurers; I understand nothing about government. But it seems strange that with all our volumes on the subject of government, from Plato to Machiavelli, we should not all be well acquainted with the duties of the heads of state and the science of government.

Many people wish changes of government. The English, who have no objection to changing ministers every eight hours, cling to their form of government itself. We are forever reminded of the admirable republics of ancient Greece. No doubt the Greeks preferred the government of Pericles and Demosthenes to that of the Turkish

50

pashas, but in their most prosperous and palmy days they were always complaining; while they gave laws to the old Romans, their own were so bad that they were continually changing them.

What could be said in favor of a government under which the just Aristides was banished, Phocion put to death, Socrates condemned to drink hemlock after having been exposed to banter and derision on the stage by Aristophanes, and under which the Amphyctions, with sad stupidity, actually delivered Greece into the power of Philip because the Phocians had ploughed up a field which was part of the territory of Apollo? But the government of the neighboring monarchies was worse.

A Swiss, a Hollander, a Venetian, an Englishman, and a Roman cardinal were once disputing, while they travelled, about their respective governments, and which of them was best. No one knew much about the matter, each stuck to his opinion without knowing very distinctly what it was, and they came to no conclusion, each praising his own country from vanity, but complaining about it from his personal bias.

Few nations are governed by themselves. It is not the English who reign in England: the king is of a German family which succeeded a Dutch prince who followed a Scotch family which had come from an Angevin family that had replaced a Norman family that had expelled a family of usurping Saxons. Rome had many emperors who were born in the barbarous provinces, and many popes born in provinces no less barbarous. Let him govern who can, and when he has become master, according to his best light.

In 1769 a traveller reported on one of the

countries he had seen in a world tour, "It had become involved with its neighbors in a war which was dubbed the Ridiculous because much was lost and nothing was gained by it. At the conclusion of peace," said the traveller, "it was in the most dreadful state of misery; it had lost money, soldiers, fleet, and commerce. It seemed a nation absolutely annihilated, and this was a pity, for a great part of the people were amiable, industrious, and gay, after an earlier period of being coarse, superstitious, and barbarous. Yet at the end of two years its capital and principal cities were more opulent than ever. Luxury had increased, and an air of enjoyment prevailed everywhere. It was only after I had examined the governments of the neighboring nations that I could discover the cause of what appeared so unaccountable. I found that those governments were just as bad as that of this nation, but that it was superior to all the rest in industry."

The insular situation of the English, setting up a need for navigation, has probably contributed to that quality in their minds which induces a character more firm, more reflective, more persevering, and perhaps more obstinate, than is to be found in some other nations.

The forthright conduct of the English, which has made their island the theatre of many a bloody tragedy, has contributed likewise to their utter frankness. Much of their royal blood has been shed in the field and on the scaffold, while poison, throughout their long and violent domestic contentions, has never been resorted to; in countries under priestly domination poison has been the favorite weapon of destruction.

The love of liberty has increased among the

English as they have advanced in knowledge and wealth. Every citizen of a state cannot be equally powerful, but he may be equally free; an understanding of this the English have attained. To be free is to be dependent only on obedience to the law. The English have ever loved law-abiding as fathers love their children, for they consider themselves the begetters of their laws.

A government of this kind is a late development. The people long were in awe of powers vested in pope, king, baron, and bishop. Then arose the House of Commons, which was in reality the nation. The king, as head of the nation, acted only for himself on what was called his prerogative; peers and bishops had a parliament only for themselves, in the same manner. But the House of Commons is for the people, as every member of it is deputed by the people. This democratic body—in comparison with which the republic of Plato is a ridiculous fantasy — came into being only as a protest against abuses which now make human nature shudder. And I cannot but believe that all states not founded upon similar principles will end in revolution.

Under the English constitution all men are restored to those natural rights which, in nearly all monarchies, they are deprived of. They have entire liberty of person and property; freedom of the press; the right of being tried in all criminal cases by a jury of independent men—the right of being tried only according to the strict letter of the law; and the right of every man to profess unmolested what religion he chooses. To be secure on lying down that you will arise still possessed of that property you had when retiring to rest; that you will not be torn from the arms of your wife, and from your children, in the dead of night, to be thrown into a dungeon, or buried in exile; that you will wake able to express all your thoughts; and that if you are accused of acting, speaking, or writing wrongly, you can be tried only according to law — these privileges are extended even to every foreigner who sets foot on English soil. I venture to assert that were the human race assembled all together for the purpose of governing itself, it would make such laws as these for its security.

Greatness

THE great man is more difficult to point out than the great artist. In an art or profession the man who has outdistanced his rivals (or who has the reputation of having done so) is called great in his work, with reservations as to his character. But the great man must exhibit different merit. It is easier to say who are not great men than who are. They should have great virtues. It is agreed that Cromwell was a most intrepid general, profound statesman, and the man best qualified to conduct the party, parliament, or army of his day, yet no writer has called him a great man because, although he possessed great qualities, he possessed not a single great virtue.

Happiness

CAN one man be happier than another? It is clear that a man who has the gout and stone, who has lost his money, his good name, his wife and family, and who is about to be hanged after having been mangled, is less happy than a young, vigorous sultan, or La Fontaine's cobbler. But how are we to determine which is the happier of two men equally healthy, prosperous, and placed in society? Their temperaments must decide it. The most moderate, the least worrisome, and the most keenly perceptive is the most happy; but unfortunately the most keenly perceptive is often the least moderate. It is not our position, but our disposition which renders us happy. Our disposition depends upon the functioning of our organs, over which we have no control.

Hell

THE poets, having invented the infernal regions, were the first to laugh at them. In the *Aeneid* Virgil sometimes mentions hell seriously because that suits his subject, and sometimes he speaks of it with contempt. Marcus Aurelius philosophically reasons, "He who fears death fears either to be deprived of all senses, or to experience new sensations. If one no longer retains his own senses he will no longer be subject to pain or grief for, being totally different, he will have senses of a different nature."

When men came to a social organization they must have perceived that a great number of criminals eluded the severity of the laws; it was necessary to establish a check; this was to be found only in religion. The Persians, Chaldaeans, Egyptians, and Greeks entertained the idea of punishments after the present life; and of all the nations of antiquity that we are acquainted with, only the Jews admitted punishment on earth alone. But among them the Pharisees and Essenians did admit, according to certain notions of their own, a belief in hell. This dogma had passed from the Greeks to the Romans and was adopted by the Christians. Yet many of the fathers of the Church rejected the doctrine of eternal punishment. It appeared to them absurd that an unfortunate man should burn throughout eternity for stealing a goat. When the time comes in which no one any longer believes in hell, what restraint will there be upon wickedness? Why, there will be a feeling of honor, and the restraint of the laws — that of the Deity Himself whose will it is that mankind be just, whether there be a hell or not.

History

HISTORY is the recital of facts represented as true. Fable, on the other hand, is the recital of facts represented as fiction. The history of man's ideas is nothing more than the chronicle of human error.

Certainty not based upon mathematical demonstration is only probability; most history must be that. When Marco Polo described the greatness and the people of China, being the first and for a time the only western writer who had described them, he was not believed. The Portuguese, who later came into communication with that vast empire through trade with it, began to make the description probable. It is now a matter of certainty, for thousands of witnesses from different nations know about it, unopposed by contrary testimony.

Periods are distinguished as either fabulous or historical. But even in historic times it is necessary to separate truth from fable. Was it very likely that Romulus, the grandson of the king of the Sabines, was compelled to carry off the Sabine women in order to get wives for his men? Is the history of the chaste Lucretia highly probable? Does the adventure of Regulus, in a hogshead stuck round with iron spikes, deserve belief? Would not Polybius, a contemporary, have recorded it had it been true?

We might naturally be led to think that a monument erected to commemorate an event would attest its certainty. Then does the famous statue of Laocoon furnish incontestable evidence of the truth of the story of the Trojan horse? One of our own most ancient monuments is a figure of St. Denis shown carrying his head in his hands. Portraits frequently show more of an inclination toward display than toward the historic record.

When the English wrote their version of the history of the war of 1741, they recorded that at the battle of Fontenoy the French fired balls and chunks of glass soaked in poison; the Duke of Cumberland sent the King of France a boxful of these marvels which had been found in the bodies of the wounded English. And, because the French were supposed to have lost forty thousand men in that battle, it was reported that an act of parliament was passed to prevent the French from talking about it. In the fraudulent memoirs of Mme. de Maintenon we are told that at the siege of Lille the allies threw leaflets into the city with the message, "Frenchmen, be comforted — Maintenon will never be your queen."

History is sometimes even more shamefully abused in England. As there are always two parties in a state of pitched battle, until some common cause unites them for a season, the writings of one faction condemn everything that the other approves. The same individual is represented as a Cato and a Cataline. Perhaps the truth may be discovered only in whatever good the party historian allows his opponents, and whatever bad he imputes to his own chiefs.

Homeland

HAS a Jew a homeland? If he is born where he is surrounded with inquisitors, who would burn him if they knew that he declined to eat bacon, and appropriate his wealth, is that his country?

Or is it Palestine, inhabited by his ancestors of old, a sterile and stony land bordered by desert, of which the Turks are at present masters? He has no country; there is not a square foot of the globe which belongs to him. Can the Armenian who passes his life wandering as a money broker through every country of the east exclaim of any place, "This is my own, my native land!"? He has no homeland but his purse and account book. The monks — what is their homeland? Heaven, they say. All in good time; but what is it now? What is a homeland, anyway? Is it not in all probability that little piece of ground with its comfortable house, of which the possessor may say, "This field that I cultivate, this house that I have built, are my own. I live under the protection of laws that no tyrant can revoke. When those of my neighbors who have fields and houses like mine assemble in the common interests, I have a voice in the assembly. I am a part of that whole, one of the community, of the sovereignty. That is my homeland!"

A young pastry cook who had been to college and could muster some phrases of Cicero one day delivered himself of a lofty sentiment expressing his love of country. "What do you mean by your country?" asked the man next door. "Is it your oven — the village where you were born and to which you will never return — the street where your parents live — the town hall where you will never be an alderman—the church of Notre Dame where you can never be so much as a choir boy, though a nitwit who happens to be a duke and archbishop gets an income of twenty-four thousand a year from it?" The pastry cook was lost for a reply.

In a country of moderate extent there may be millions without a homeland. How about you, sybaritic Parisian, who have never travelled further than to Dieppe (for the sea food), who divide your time between a lush town house and a pretty villa in the country, who sit in a box at the opera that everybody but you thinks boring, who speak your own language well enough but know no other, who love your champagne from Rheims and your rents collectable semiannually? You say you love your country, but have you a homeland?

Can a financier love his homeland? Can Attila, or any one of a hundred other such heroes, always on the move, at home everywhere, have a homeland? The first who observed that any land where one prospers is one's own, was, I believe, Euripides in his *Phaedo*. But the first man who left home to seek his fortune elsewhere said it before him.

A country is made up of many families; families have self-love or esteem which extends to their town, their province, and ultimately their country, when it is called love of country. Yet the bigger a country becomes, the less can we really love it, for love spread far grows thin. One can't love all a family when it is so numerous that its members can scarcely be known.

He who burns with the ambition to be edile, tribune, praetor, consul, or dictator, claims to love his country while he loves only himself. We all want to rest snug at home, knowing that nobody can dispossess us. We want to be sure of our property and our life. Thus, with everybody having the same wishes, the individual becomes the collective interest. We speak of the welfare of the republic, meaning, of course, our own.

Which is best, a monarchy or a republic? The rich will tell you an aristocracy, the people, a democracy; only kings prefer royalty. Why then is so much of the earth still ruled by monarchs? Put the question to the mice who wanted to hang a bell on the cat. The truth is that men are rarely capable of governing themselves.

It is lamentable that good patriots must be enemies to those in other countries, for good patriots wish their countries to be enriched by commerce and victorious in arms—at the expense of their neighbors. He who would possess a true homeland must become a citizen of the world.

Ignorance

SOME there are who are so ashamed of all they do not know that they strive to disguise themselves either as wits or philosophers.

Why do we live? Why is there life? What is awareness? How do I happen to have it? How can my ear translate the vibration of air into the sensation of sound, or my eye the freighting of light into color? Of the basic mystery of all this I am profoundly ignorant, and shall always be.

What is thought? Where does it lodge? How does it happen? How do my thoughts take shape while I dream? Do I think because I will to do so? No, for as I dream, and often while I am awake, my ideas run counter to what I would have them. Ideas long forgotten and put away in the attic of my memory suddenly come to light without any effort or volition of mine, often when I had long searched in vain for them.

Why has man, of all the species of animals,

alone the mad ambition to dominate his fellows? Why do so many invite death in the attempt to satisfy this ambition?

How is it that reason is the gift we consider so precious that none of us would give it up for all the position and property in the world, while we know that it is almost always responsible for making us the most miserable of beings? Why do we, with all our passionate insistence on truth, continue to be taken in by the most palpable impostures?

Why do the vast numbers in India, deceived and enslaved by their bonzes, in subjugation to the descendant of a Tartar, bowed down by labor, groaning in misery, assailed by disease, and a mark for all the scourges of famine and plague, still cling fondly to life? Whence comes evil; why does it exist?

O my fellow atoms of a day! O my comrades in littleness, born like me to suffer everything and be ignorant of everything! Are there really among you any so completely deluded that you imagine you know the answers to all these questions? No; in the bottom of your hearts you can feel your own nothingness, as completely as do I. But still you are arrogant and conceited enough to wish us to embrace your vain systems; not having the power to tyrannize over our bodies, you aspire to become the tyrants of our spirit!

Impotence

THE canon law made considerable to-do of the question of impotence. Might a man who was prevented by sorcery from consummating his marriage, after being divorced and having children by a second wife — might he, on the death of the second, still reject his first wife should she lay claim to him? All the great canonists decided in the negative: Alexander de Nevo, Andrew Alberic, Turrecremata, Soto, and fifty more.

It is impossible to help admiring the sagacity exhibited by the canonists, especially for the knowledge those irreproachable celibates had of the mysteries of sexual intercourse. There is no aberration, however strange, on which they did not hold forth. They discussed at length all the cases in which capability may exist at one time or in one situation, and impotence in another. They inquired into all the ingenious devices to assist nature, and with the avowed object of pronouncing what is allowable and what is not, exposed all which might have remained veiled.

Sanchez especially distinguished himself by collecting cases of conscience which the boldest wife would hesitate to submit to her most prudent confidante. One query led to another in interminable succession, until the ultimate was reached in the extraordinary examination of the manner of communication of the Holy Ghost with the Virgin Mary. Such exhaustive researches had never before been made, and could never have been made save by theologians.

In the Gospels divorce is spoken of as allowable for adultery alone. Jewish law permitted a husband to repudiate a wife who displeased him, without specifying the cause—"if she found no favor in his eyes." This law says nothing of impotence. It would appear, remarks a casuist, that God provided no impotence among a people who were to multiply like the sands on the shore, and to inherit the vast territory between the Nile and the Euphrates, indeed, to become lords of the earth. To fulfill divine promises, every honest Jew would have to labor unceasingly at the great work of propagation. There was certainly a curse upon impotence. The time had not yet arrived for the devout to live as eunuchs for the kingdom of heaven.

Marriage having arrived in the course of time at the dignity of a sacrament and mystery, the ecclesiastics naturally became judges of all which took place between husband and wife, and not only that, but also all which did *not* take place.

Wives possessed the right to present a request to be *embesognées*—the French term, though the proceedings were carried on in Latin. Clerks pleaded and priests pronounced judgment, to determine these points: whether a man was bewitched — or a woman merely wanted another husband.

The most important proof of capability required from persons accused of impotence was that called "the congress." This combat in an enclosed field was adopted in France in the fourteenth century; Bouhier asserts that it was known nowhere else. It was not conducted exactly as people have imagined. It was supposed that a conjugal consummation took place under the inspection of physicians, surgeons, and midwives, but such was not the case. The parties went to bed in the usual manner, and at a proper time the inspectors, who waited in the next room, were called in to pronounce upon the case.

In the famous process of the Marquis de Langeais, decided in 1659, he demanded the congress; but thanks to the management of his lady, Marie de St. Simon, did not succeed. He demanded a second trial but the judges, tired of the outcries of the superstitious, the plaints of the prudes, and the raillery of the wits, refused it. They declared the marquis impotent and his marriage void, forbade him to marry again, and allowed his wife to take another husband. He disregarded this sentence, married Diana de Navailles, and by her had seven children!

Incubi

HAVE there ever been incubi and succubi? If you doubt it, our learned jurisconsults and demonologists have proved both to exist.

It is supposed that Satan, always a very busy person, spends time producing heated dreams in young ladies and gentlemen, and by a sort of double process achieves the same end which resulted in so many heroes and demigods of old. He certainly took superfluous trouble, for he could have left the young people alone, and without his assistance the world would have been sufficiently supplied with heroes.

The ancient gods frequently disguised themselves, in the pursuit of human girls, as eagles, pigeons, swans, horses, or showers of gold, but the goddesses assumed no disguise, having only to show themselves to gain their objective. It is presumed that, whatever shapes the gods assumed, they consummated their loves in the convenient and more compatible form of men.

In accepting a demonistic scheme (less noble and decorous than that of the deities of antiquity) we believed a girl might be rendered pregnant by the ministry of the devil. We cannot doubt that this is possible, for the Sorbonne decided it to be true in 1318, and the decision has never been revoked. We are bound to believe in incubi and succubi, because our professors have evidently always believed in them. And not only they. Bodin, in his book about sorcerers, tells of Jean Hervilier, a native of Verberie, who was condemned by the Parliament of Paris to be burned alive for having prostituted his daughter to the devil. We learn that the embraces of this personage, who appeared as a big black man, were attended with a sensation of cold, which would seem rather contrary to his constitution.

The celebrated Picus of Mirandola—a prince never lies—says he knew an old man of eighty who had slept half his life with a female demon, and another of seventy who had enjoyed a similar felicity. Both are buried at Rome. That proves beyond doubt the existence of incubi and succubi.

At least it is impossible to disprove it. If a demon can enter our bodies, why can he not take the same liberty with our wives and daughters? If there are demons, there must of course be demonesses. For the one to beget children on our women, there must be the other for us to use likewise. The empire of the devil is indeed universal. Or was until reason unthroned him.

Instinct

By instinct we do many involuntary things, just as it is our instinct to have curiosity, to run after novelty and away from danger, to be vexed by contempt, appeased by an air of submission, and softened by tears.

Like cats and goats we are governed by instinct, but ours is not so shrewd and developed as theirs. The newly born calf or lamb seeks its mother's milk at once, while the human infant, unless taken to the breast, would inevitably perish.

No pregnant woman was ever impelled by instinct to prepare a wicker cradle for her child, as the wren prepares a nest. But the power of thought which we possess, together with the industrious hands we are given by nature, raises us to equality with animals and their instinct, and in the course of time places us far above them in our capabilities for good and evil — a proposition condemned by the French parliament and the Sorbonne.

It is our instinct which drives us to beat our brother when he angers us, if we are sent into a rage—and feel ourselves stronger than he. Thenceforward it is our sublime reason which leads us to the devices of arrows, swords, pikes, and firearms to kill him with.

Instinct urges us to *make* love but Virgil, Tibullus, and Ovid *sing* it. Instinct causes the industrious apprentice to gaze with respect and admiration at the fine glistening coach of a commissioner of taxes. Then reason comes into play. He rises to be a commissioner himself, he learns the ins and outs of tax collecting, he embezzles, becomes a great man in his turn, and dazzles his erstwhile associates as he rides by lolling in his own coach, more richly gilded than the one which first roused his ambition.

What is this instinct which governs the whole animal kingdom, and which in man may be aided by reason or may be repressed by habit? It is something divine. Everything is swayed or impelled by nature. We reason about everything, creating nothing.

Justice

THAT justice is often extremely unjust is more than a present-day observation. *Summum jus, summa injuria,* is one of the most ancient of proverbs. There are many dreadful ways of being unjust. An innocent man may be racked on equivocal evidence. A man may be condemned to execution when he deserves no more than three months' imprisonment. Such injustice is meted out by tyrants, and particularly by fanatics, who always become tyrants when they are given power to do mischief.

Kissing

PARDON me, young ladies and gentlemen. In this article you won't find what you are looking for. It is only for scholarly and serious people, to whom I fear it can be of little practical use.

There is too much kissing in the comedies of Molière's time. There valets are always asking soubrettes for a kiss. This gets pretty flat and un-

amusing when the actors are nothing to look at anyway. John de la Casa, archbishop of Benevento, in his chapter on kissing, sanctions it from head to foot, but deplores long noses, and advises ladies who have them to choose flat-nosed lovers.

Throughout ancient times the kiss was the usual salutation. Plutarch relates that the conspirators, before they killed Caesar, kissed his face, hands, and breast. Tacitus observes that when his father-in-law, Agricola, came from Rome, Domitian kissed him coldly, said nothing to him, and left him confounded in the crowd. An inferior, who could not aspire to giving a kiss, kissed his own hand, and the superior returned it in the same way if he deigned to.

The kiss is a ceremony in worship. Job in his parable says that he has not adored the sun and moon like the other Arabs, nor has his mouth kissed his hand to them. Nothing remains of this custom in Europe save in country places where children are still taught to kiss their right hands by way of thanking for the gift of a sweet.

It is particularly reprehensible to betray by a kiss — witness that of Judas. One of the captains of David, Joab, being jealous of another captain, Amasa, said, "Art thou in health, my brother?" took him by the beard with the right hand as if to kiss him, and with the other drew his sword and disembowelled him. I cannot cite another instance of kissing in assassination (itself so frequent among the Jews) save possibly that of Judith before she cut off the head of Holofernes in bed; it is not actually mentioned, but is probable enough. In Shakespeare's *Othello* the Moor gives his wife two kisses before smothering her. To sedate persons this seems quite dreadful, but adherents of Shakespeare cite it as a fine touch of realism, especially for a Moor.

The early Christians of both sexes kissed at their *agapae* or love feasts. They bestowed the holy kiss, the kiss of peace, and the brotherly and sisterly kiss. Though it lasted four centuries, this custom was finally abolished in distrust of the consequences. It drew on the Christians, when they were little known, imputations of debauchery from the priests of Jupiter and the priestesses of Vesta. We read in Petronius and other authors that dissolute Romans called one another brother and sister, and it was assumed that the Christians did so with no better intent. Innocently they gave occasion for scandal about themselves.

Among the primitive Christians there were seventeen societies. Those which considered themselves most orthodox accused the others of all sorts of impurity. St. Epiphanius in the third century claimed that the men and women of the gnostics — at first an honorable term signifying the learned, enlightened, and pure, but which became an epithet of horror and contempt, and a reproach of heresy—proceeded from tickling each other to lascivious kisses, judging by their warmth the degree of faith in each other. A Christian husband, in presenting his wife to a newly-initiated member, would exort her to receive him with utmost faith, and was always obeyed. I dare not repeat, even in French, all that Epiphanius adds in Greek. But I believe that this saint was somewhat taken in, allowing himself to be carried away by his zeal, and that all heretics were not necessarily dreadful debauchees.

Kissing has long been the approved manner of greeting ladies in France, Italy, Germany, and

England. Cardinals enjoyed the privilege of kissing the lips of queens, even in Spain, though — strangely enough — not in France, where ladies have always been given greater liberties than elsewhere. But every country has its ceremonies, and there is no custom so general but that it may chance to have exceptions. It was an incivility, a mark of rudeness, in receiving the first visit of a nobleman, if a lady did not kiss his lips—even if he had a mustache. "It is an unpleasant custom," says Montaigne, "and offensive to ladies to have to present their lips to the three valets in his suite, no matter how obnoxious they may be." Old customs are old customs; I would not have them fall into disuse.

There is a grave danger to be noted. A system of nerves connects the lips to the heart and lower regions; a kiss is therefore an especially dangerous sensation. Virtue may well suffer from a prolonged and ardent kiss between two young pietists of eighteen.

It is remarkable that only mankind and turtledoves practice kissing — from the latter comes the Latin word *columbatim,* which cannot very well be rendered in our language. We cannot properly dwell longer on this interesting subject, although Montaigne remarks, "It should be discussed without reserve; we speak right out of killing, wounding, betraying, while of this we whisper."

Laughter

NOBODY doubts that laughter is a sign of joy, as tears are of grief. Those who seek the metaphysical causes of laughter crack no smile, and those who know that it is caused by a contraction of the zygomatic muscles toward the ears are doubtless very learned. Other animals have these muscles too, but neither laugh nor shed tears. The stag, to be sure, drops moisture from its eyes in an extremity of distress, as does a dog dissected alive; but they do not weep for their mistresses or friends as we do. They do not break out into guffaws at the sight of anything droll. Man is the only animal that laughs and weeps.

As we weep only when we are afflicted, and laugh only when we are gay, it has been reasoned that laughter springs from a feeling of superiority. It is true that man, a risible animal, is also a proud one; but pride does not produce laughter. A child laughing merrily does not feel himself superior to what excites his mirth — especially when he laughs from being tickled. At eleven

when I first read Molière's *Amphitryon* I roared
with laughter, but I didn't then feel superior to
Molière as a playwright. We laugh when alone,
but are seldom proud without an audience.

Not every joy produces laughter; our greatest
pleasures — love, ambition, avarice — are gravely
indulged .We grin at those who promise wonders
and perform absurdities; this is nearer hooting
than laughter.

Laws

DURING the reigns of Vespasian and Titus, when
the Romans were grilling and roasting the Jews,
a rich Israelite fled with all the gold he had accu-
mulated at his profession of usury, taking his
whole family, consisting of his wife, then far
advanced in years, his son, his daughter, two
eunuchs who were servants, one acting as cook
and the other as gardener and handyman, and a
pious Essenian, who knew the Pentateuch completely by heart, who served as his almoner. They
embarked, traversed the sea commonly called
Red (though it isn't), and entered the Persian
Gulf searching for the land of Ophir, without
knowing just where it was. A terrific storm arose,
driving their ship toward the coast of India, and
it was wrecked on one of the Maldive Islands,
now called Padrabranca, though it was then
uninhabited.

The old usurer and his wife were drowned;
only the son and daughter, the two eunuchs, and
the almoner were saved. They salvaged as much
of the provisions from the wreck as they could,
built little huts on the island, and lived there not

inconveniently and uncomfortably. As you know, the island of Padrabranca is within five degrees of the equator, and produces the largest cocoanuts and finest pineapples in the world. It was pleasant to have such an idyllic asylum when the chosen people of God were elsewhere exposed to persecution and massacre.

The Essenian could not, however, refrain from tears at the thought that they, on their happy island, were the only Jews remaining on earth, and that the seed of Abraham was therefore to be annihilated.

"In that case," said the young Jew, "its restoration is up to you; marry my sister."

"I would willingly," said the almoner, "but it is against the law. I am an Essenian; I have made a vow never to marry; the law enjoins the strictest observance of a vow; the Jewish race may come to an end, if it must; but I will certainly not marry your sister to prevent it, beautiful and amiable as she is."

"My two eunuchs," mused the Jew, "can be of no help in this. Therefore I suppose I'll have to marry her myself, if you have no objection. Please bestow the usual marriage benediction."

"I had a hundred times rather be grilled and roasted by the Roman soldiers," cried the almoner, "than to cause the committing of incest!"

"I grant you," replied the young man, "that it would be a crime at Jerusalem, where I'd have plenty of other young women to marry. But on the island of Padrabranca, where I have only cocoanuts, pineapples, and oysters, the case seems quite allowable."

The Jew accordingly married his sister and had a daughter by her, despite the protestations of

75

the Essenian. After fourteen years the mother died without other issue, and the father said to the almoner, "Have you outgrown your old prejudices now? Will you marry my daughter?"

"God preserve me from it!" exclaimed the Essenian.

"Then," said the father, "in order to preserve the seed of Abraham, I suppose I'll have to marry her myself."

Struck with inexpressible horror, the Essenian, resolving to stay no longer where the law was twice violated, plunged into the water.

"Come back, come back!" called the father. "I am only obeying the law of nature and doing good for my homeland."

But the almoner swam and swam without looking back. At length he reached another island, Attola, which was highly populous and civilized. The moment he crawled ashore he was seized and made a slave.

He protested against this inhospitable treatment, but he was assured that it was the law. Ever since Attola had been nearly surprised by a hostile landing of the people of Ada, it had been wisely enacted that all strangers landing there were to be made slaves. Fortunately he was given to a kind and wealthy master who treated him very well, and to whom he became strongly attached.

One night some murderers came to his house, to kill the master and carry off his treasure. They asked the slaves where he was, and where he kept his money. "On our oath," said the other slaves, "we don't know." But the Essenian spoke up, "Lying is unlawful. The master is here, and he has a lot of money hidden in the house."

76

So the master was robbed and murdered. And when they were haled before a judge, the slaves accused the Essenian of having betrayed their master. He said that nothing in the world could have induced him to tell a lie; and he was hanged.

Libel

SMALL offensive books are termed libels. They are usually small because the authors, having few reasons to give, writing not to inform but to mislead, and wanting to be read, must necessarily be brief. They are usually anonymous; assassins are afraid of being caught with contraband weapons.

For eighteen hundred years we have been having theological libels—all the worse for being considered sacred by the uninquiring.

Boileau and Fontenelle, in the midst of their battle of epigrams, spread the report that they would have to move to larger quarters to house all the libels they had received. Some would go so far as to say that anything offensive written against a neighbor is libel.

The attacks of the prophets on the kings of Israel have been considered no better than rabble-rousing libels. It is doubtful if they really did any great harm. People seldom read. Sedition is not stirred up by writing pamphlets, though direct speech to the mob has its effect. On her accession one of the first things done by Queen Elizabeth of England was to muzzle the pulpit; she let no one preach without getting permission for what he was going to say.

But if you really want fair specimens of libel, look at some of the manifestoes of sovereigns.

Liberty

A. SUPPOSE a battery of cannon is discharged at us; have you the liberty to hear it or not, as you please?

B. I can't help but hear it!

A. Would you consent to have your head taken off by those cannon?

B. What a question!

A. Then you have neither the power of not hearing, nor the power of staying within range.

B. Granted.

A. Then what is liberty save the power of following the body's will?

B. Why, in that case, my hunting dog is as free as I am. He has the will to run when he sees a hare, and the power of running if there is nothing the matter with his legs. I am no better than my dog; you've put me on a level with the beasts.

A. You are unwilling to be free like your dog? Don't you eat, sleep, and propagate as he does? Why is your liberty different from his?

B. I have a soul and reason; my dog scarcely reasons at all. He has nothing beyond simple ideas, while I have a thousand metaphysical ones.

A. Well, you may be a thousand times freer, but not free any differently.

B. I am free to will as I like!

A. Only according to ideas you have somehow absorbed. For example, what if I asked you whether you wanted to get married or not?

B. What if I answered, neither the one or the other?

A. Then you'd be like the fellow who declared, "Some believe the Cardinal Mazarin is dead, some believe he's still alive; I believe neither the one nor the other."

B. Well, for the sake of the argument, I want to get married.

A. Good. Why?

B. Because I'm in love. She's a young, beautiful, sweet girl. She's well brought up; she's rich. She can sing. Her parents are nice people. She loves me and her family approves of me.

A. There, you see all the reasons! You can't will a thing without motives. I say, when you are free to marry, you have the power to sign the license, attend the ceremony, and sleep with your wife.

B. But not without motives? I'm not really free?

A. Your will isn't but your actions are. You are free to act when you have the power to.

B. Maybe you're right. I'll think about it.

Love

THERE are so many kinds of love that, in defining it, one must be specific. Some apply the term to a caprice of a few days, a connection without attachment, a passion without affection, a pretense, a gallantry, a mere ceremony, a romantic fancy, a taste followed quickly by distaste. It is applied to innumerable fantasies.

Should a philosopher be inclined to make an exhaustive research into a subject so unphilosophical, he might begin with Plato's *Symposium*, wherein Socrates, the decent and honorable lover of Alcibiades and Agathon, converses with them on the metaphysics of love. Lucretius speaks of it as a natural philosopher, and so does Virgil.

It is an imaginative embroidery on the stuff of nature. Look at the sparrows in your garden; see your doves; observe the bull as he meets the heifer; regard that powerful, spirited stallion which a couple of your grooms are leading to the mare that quietly waits, evidently pleased at his approach; catch the flash in his eye, hear his resonant, melodious neighing, notice his springing and curveting, his pointed ears, his mouth open and convulsively gasping, his distended nostrils, his fiery breath, his erect, waving mane, and the impetuous dash with which he rushes toward what nature has destined for him; do not, however, envy him his pleasure, but reflect on the advantages which the human species have in love, as a compensation for the strength, beauty, lightness, and celerity of mere animals.

Most of the animals which copulate take pleasure through but a single sense; when appetite is satisfied, all is over. No animal but man knows fondling; his whole body is sensitive to it; his lips particularly experience an unwearying delight which belongs to his species alone; finally, he is alive to the endearments of love at all seasons, while mere animals know them only for limited periods. If you reflect on this lofty preëminence, you will agree with the Earl of Rochester's remark that love would impel a whole nation of atheists to worship God.

As men have a faculty of perfecting what nature has bestowed, they have improved upon the gift of love. Cleanliness, good care, and health render the body more sensitive and increase its capacity for pleasure. All amiable and estimable qualities merge into love, as metals amalgamate with gold; friendship and respect rally to its support; excellence both of mind and body strengthen its bonds.

Such are the advantages possessed by man over the animals. But if he has pleasures unknown to them, how many pains does he have that they are free of! The most dreadful of these come from

a disease to which man alone is subject, which has poisoned the pleasures of love and sources of life over most of the globe. This is not, like other maladies, a consequence of excess. It was not introduced through debauchery. The Phrynes and Laïses, the Floras and Messalinas, never had it. It originated in islands where man dwelt in innocence, whence it has spread throughout the civilized world. If nature could be accused of despising her own work, thwarting her own scheme, and quarreling with her own impulses it would be in this horrible scourge. And can this, then, be in the best of all possible worlds? If Caesar and Anthony and Octavius never had the disease, why should Francis I have died of it? Things seem to be so ordered—unfortunately for those to whom Rabelais dedicated his book.

Marriage

ONCE I met a motto merchant who recited some of his best stock items: "Induce citizens to marry as early as possible. Let them be tax-exempt the first year, passing on their assessments to those of the same age who remain unmarried.

"The more married men there are, the fewer will be the crimes. Look at the criminal court news: you'll see a hundred youths indicted to one father of a family.

"Marriage makes a man wiser and more virtuous. The father of a family hesitates to make a fool of himself before his children, or to give them shame for their inheritance.

"Let soldiers marry; they will no longer desert. Bound to their families, they are bound to their country. An unmarried soldier is often nothing but a vagabond, caring little whether he serves the King of Naples or of Morocco."

Roman soldiers were married. They fought for their wives and children and made slaves of the wives and children of other nations.

A great Italian politician, who knew several oriental languages — something our own politicians seldom do — said to me when I was young, "*Caro figlio,* remember that the Jews had one pretty good practice: they abhorred virginity. If that superstitious little nation of jobbers hadn't regarded marriage as the first of human obligations, if they had set up convents of nuns, they would surely have been goners."

St. Augustine approved marriages of the orthodox with heretics, for he hoped that the faithful spouse would convert the other; and Louis XIV condemned them, lest the heterodox should pervert the believer.

Miracles

A LEARNED Jesuit, for many years a missionary in the Indies, deplored the fact that neither he nor any of his colleagues had ever been able to perform a miracle. On the other hand Xavier, who lamented that he had not the gift of languages, who went among the Japanese, as he said, like a dumb statue, is recorded to have resuscitated eight persons. That was no small matter, though to be sure it was a few thousand miles away. Since then there have been people who expressed themselves as considering the abolition of the Jesuits in France, at the time during which it was effected, as a much greater miracle than any performed by Xavier or Ignatius.

A philosopher was once asked what he would say if he were to see the sun stand still, the dead rise again, the mountains slip into the sea, and such wonders, all to prove some important truth such as, for instance, divine wisdom. "What would I say?" repeated the philosopher. "I would say that one thing contradicted the other."

In order to believe a miracle it is not enough merely to have seen it; the senses may be deceived. A fool is often called a dealer in wonders. Not only do many worthy people think they have seen what they have not seen and hear what they have not heard, but they find miracles being worked on them. They are cured of vapors by supernatural power. They even change into wolves, sail through the air on broomsticks, and become incubi and succubi.

A miracle must be seen by a number of people in full possession of health and their senses, who are quite disinterested in its occurrence. They should, moreover, attest it solemnly. If there must be signatures to simple transactions such as selling a house or making a will, what cautionary formalities are not necessary to verify something which is naturally impossible, and upon which the destiny of the world might depend?

Even when an authentic miracle is performed, it may prove nothing. The Scriptures warn that impostors may work miracles and that if someone, working them, should proclaim another God than that of the Jews, he should be stoned to death. It is therefore requisite that doctrine be confirmed by miracle, and miracle by doctrine. But even this is not enough. Impostors may preach morality which is altogether pure and correct, the better to deceive. Impostors like the magicians of Pharaoh performed miracles.

A theocracy can be founded only upon miracles. The Great Sovereign speaks to men only in prodigies. These are his ministers and letters patent. His orders are intimated by the waters of the ocean rising to drown nations, or by them opening so that one may pass through them on dry land. In Jewish history, you see, everything is miraculous from the creation of Adam to the time of the insignificant little monarch Saul. Thenceforward theocracy shares place with royalty, though miracles still come to pass from time to time; no longer, however, in that splendid train of prodigies which continually astonish and interrupt nature.

The cleverest work ever to be written against miracles and prophecies was that of Lord Bolingbroke. Happily it is so voluminous, so destitute of method, so verbose, and so abounding in long and sometimes complicated sentences, that few have had the patience to read it.

A number of writers, whose misfortune it was to be philosophers rather than Christians, have been bold enough to deny the miracles of our Lord. Let us lament these unhappy men, led astray by their own deceitful reason and cast into their own hopeless abyss.

Money

In the thirteenth, fourteenth, and fifteenth centuries the papal treasury undoubtedly had the most ready money of any in Europe. All Europe sent its money to the Roman court, which gave in exchange consecrated beads, agnuses, indulgences plenary and limited, dispensations, confirmations, exemptions, benedictions, and even excommunications—against whomsoever the subscriber chose, or had not sufficient faith in the goods of the court.

What became of the money which shortly thereafter flowed into Spain from Mexico and Peru? It entered the pockets of the French, English, and Dutch, who traded with Cadiz under Spanish names, and sent their manufactured products back to America. Much of this money then went to the Indies to pay for spices, cotton, saltpetre, sugar, confections, tea, fabrics, diamonds, and monkeys. And what became of it in the Indies? Some was buried in the earth, and predatory leaders made use of the rest to raise troops against one another. For, as Caesar so truly remarks, "With money we get soldiers, and with soldiers we steal money."

How did the ancient Romans in the time of Romulus ever get along? They hadn't so much as a sou in their pockets (nor pockets, for that matter); our very coachmen have gold watches that the seven kings of Rome could not have paid for. If a Manlius, Curius, or Fabius of ancient Rome should have come afoot to the house of our receiver-general of finances, not of course having wherewithal to take part in the gaming, the receiver-general's lady, having this article read to her at her toilette by the bel-esprit of the ménage, would not have allowed him to enter her antechamber.

What has made some of our sharper scholars suspect that the Pentateuch was not written until the era when the Jews began to get coins from their neighbors is the fact that in more than one passage mention is made of shekels. And that brings me to the riches of Solomon. They are variously computed as having been twenty-one, twenty-two, or twenty-five million; and while the grand Turk's keeper of treasure cannot hazard a guess at how much it really was, we have several young bachelors of theology at Oxford and the Sorbonne who can tell you the amount without hesitation.

Through its innumerable adventures of being stamped, marked, valued, clipped, multiplied, buried, and stolen, money has always remained the idol of mankind.

It is so much loved among Christian princes that there is still in force an old law which prohibits sending gold and silver out of the country. This law implies one of two things: that the princes reign over fools who lavish their money for pleasure in foreign countries, or that we must never pay our debt abroad.

Speaking of government, does not its art lie in taking as much money as possible from one group of citizens to give it to another?

Morality

I HAVE just read in a fourteen-volume history, "The Christians had a morality, but the pagans had none." What nonsense; what of the morality of Socrates, of Zaleucus, of Charondas, of Cicero, of Epictetus, and of Marcus Aurelius?

There is but one morality, as there is but one geometry. You say that most men know little about geometry. True; but if they study it ever so little, they all draw the same conclusions. Farmers, factory hands, laborers, do not take courses in morality; they read neither Cicero's *De Finibus* nor Aristotle's *Ethics,* yet the moment they start to think they are disciples of Cicero. The Indian dyer, the Tartar shepherd, and the English sailor know justice and injustice. Confucius did not invent a system of morals; he found it in the hearts of mankind.

There is no morality in superstition. There is none in ceremonial. It has nothing to do with dogma. Dogmas differ, but morality is the same among all men who make use of their reason. Morality proceeds from God, like light; superstition is only darkness. Reflect, reader: consider the truth, and form your conclusions.

Mountain

THE fable of the mountain which after terrifying the whole countryside with its screams of labor pain, brought forth, to the ridicule of all, a mouse, is an ancient one and a universal. But those who ridiculed it were not philosophers.

Rather than mocking they should have admired. A mountain being delivered of a mouse is quite as extraordinary, quite as worthy of admiration, as a mouse being delivered of a mountain. A rock producing a rat—even that would have been prodigious; the world has never seen anything to approach it. All the constellations in the universe could not bring forth a fly. And so, where the stupid mock, the philosopher marvels; where the insensitive stare in astonishment, he often smiles.

Nakedness

WHY do we hasten to lock up a man found naked in the streets, when we take no offence at statues in the same state, or paintings of Jesus and Mary Magdalen to be seen in certain churches? It is probable that man got along for a good while before he discovered raiment. In more than one South Sea island, and in America, there are still people ignorant of the art of the tailor.

The more civilized primitive peoples deck their privy parts with leaves, rushwork, and feathers. Is this the concealment of modesty or the veiling of what nature provokes our desire to discover? In even more polished levels of culture there are sects which, in worshipping God, deprive themselves of clothing. Such have been the Adamites and the Abelians, who assembled naked to sing the praises of God. We have this on the word of St. Epiphanius and St. Augustine, who were not, to be sure, contemporaries, and who lived a distance away. This folly is just as possible as a hundred others which have made their trips around the world.

There are saints of Islam who go about bare as apes. It is possible that such madmen think it more proper to present themselves before the Deity as He made them, than under disguises of their own invention. They may have exposed themselves in an ecstasy of chastity, for there are so few well-made specimens of either sex that nakedness does nothing to arouse desire.

It is also recorded that the Abelians renounced marriage. If they had very many lusty youths or amorous maidens, they could not have been too much like St. Adhelm or the happy Robert D'Arbriselle, who lay with the most luscious of ladies only to prove the strength of their continence.

I must confess to thinking that it must have been pleasant to see a hundred naked Helens and Parises singing anthems, giving one another the kiss of peace, and performing the ceremonies of the agapae.

Nature

PHILOSOPHER. What are you, nature? I live in you. I have been seeking you these fifty years. Yet I have never found you.

NATURE. The ancient Egyptians who lived to be twelve hundred years old, confronted me with the same reproach. They called me Isis and placed so impenetrable a veil over me that none could peer through.

P. For that very reason I come to you directly. I have been able to measure your planets, to ascertain their courses, and to point out the laws of their motion. But what are you yourself? Are you active? Are you passive? What is the order of

your elements? Have you an all-embracing intelligence, as bodies of men who meet have opinions,
unperceived by the individual?

N. I am no mathematician yet everything
within me conforms to mathematical laws.

P. But there must be an eternal geometrician
who directs you.

N. I am water, earth, fire, air, animal, vegeta-
ble, mineral. I perceive the intelligence that is in
me though I cannot see it. Then why should you,
so minute a part of me, be anxious to know what
I myself know not?

P. Curiosity! I want to know why your coarse-
textured mountains and deserts differ so much
from your delicate-fibered plants and animals.

N. Listen, I'll tell you a secret. Really I am not
Nature at all; the wrong name was given me; I
am Art.

P. Mother, tell me why we exist!

N. I can give you only the answer that I have
given for ages: I know nothing whatsoever of
the matter.

P. Why are successions of creatures repro-
duced, to devour and be devoured? Why do they
have sensation, to endure so much pain? Why do
those who can reason avail themselves so little
of the faculty? What was the purpose of all this?

N. You must go and ask that of Him who made
me.

Novelty

THE first words of OVID'S *Metamorphoses*, "In
nova fert animus," might be taken as the motto
of mankind. Nobody gets very much excited by

the wonderful spectacle of sunrise, which can be seen every day, but a lot of people run to gape at the smallest meteor that plummets through the autumn sky. We despise what is common or what has long been known. Shops will not burden themselves with Virgil or Horace, only with the latest best sellers, no matter how bad. And the clerks take you aside and say, "We've just got in a shipment from abroad."

Women have ever complained that men desert them for what has no merit but its novelty. And ladies — I regret to say, for I have infinite respect for them—give men the same cause to complain.

Perhaps this widespread hunger for novelty is a benefit of nature. We are told, "Be content with what you have. Desire no more than you deserve. Quell your restless spirits." These are good maxims. But if we had followed them we should still be feeding on acorns and sleeping under the stars, and should have had no Corneille, Racine, Molière, or Voltaire.

Optimism

CAN you explain to me, gentlemen, why everything is for the best? This is too much for me. Does it mean that everything is disposed and ordered according to the laws of inevitability? That I understand and acknowledge. Does it mean that everyone is well if he is alive—that nobody suffers? You'll grant that such is not the case. Do you think that the sorry mishaps which befall the earth are good in some way of God's, that He takes pleasure in them? I cannot accept this horrible doctrine, and neither can you.

Acording to Plato, Divinity chose the best of all possible worlds. This tenet has been accepted by many Christian philosophers, although it seems at cross-purposes with the doctrine of original sin. After the fall, this was no longer the best of all possible worlds. If it was ever so it might still be so; but many think it the worst of worlds instead of the best.

Leibnitz takes the part of Plato. Since readers complain that one is no clearer than the other, and I who have read them both more than once must agree with them; and since the gospel reveals nothing on the subject, I do not feel too badly at having to remain in the dark.

To be driven out of a delightful garden where we might have lived forever if only an apple hadn't been eaten — to bring forth poor children into misery, only that they may bring forth more — to be sick with so many diseases, vexed with so many disappointments, to die amidst grief, and in recompense to burn throughout eternity — is this the best of all possible lots? It certainly isn't good, so far as we are concerned; then how can it be so to God? Leibnitz makes no reply to these objections; he merely makes books, which I fear he himself does not understand.

Lucullus, aglow with health, sharing a good dinner with his friends and mistresses in the hall of Apollo, may lightly deny the existence of evil. But let him put his head out of the window and he can see wretches aplenty; let him be taken with fever, and he will be one himself.

I dislike quoting; it is full of pitfalls. Passages are too often cited out of context, and misconceptions ensue. But I must quote the early Christian father Lactantius, who in his chapter on the anger

93

of God causes Epicurus to speak thus: "God can either take evil from the world and will not; or, being willing to do so, cannot; or He neither can nor will; or, last, He is both able and willing. If He is willing to take evil and cannot, He is not omnipotent. If He can but will not He is not benevolent. If He is neither able nor willing He is neither powerful nor benevolent. Finally, if He is both able and willing, how can evil exist?"

The origin of evil has always been a knotty problem. Thus many ancient philosophers resorted to a belief in two equal powers of good and evil. Not the least of absurdities is the presumption that two all-powerful beings, locked in the struggle for the world, should make a treaty like that of the two quacks in Molière, "Give me the clyster and I'll let you have the lancet."

Basilides maintained, with the Neoplatonists of the first century of the Church, that God gave the making of the world to some of His inferior angels who, being inexpert, produced what we have. This theological fable is brushed aside by the objection that it is not in the nature of a Deity all-powerful and all-wise to entrust the construction of a world to subcontractors, incompetent at that. Simon, sensing this objection, obviates it by saying that the slovenly angel was sent to damnation for his work; but roasting an angel makes no amends.

Pandora's adventure, as the Greeks told it, offers no better solution. The box in which all evil is stored, at the bottom of which remains hope, is indeed a charming allegory; but Pandora was merely fabricated by Vulcan to avenge himself on Prometheus, who had stolen fire from him to help man.

94

The Syrians had a pretty story about man and woman, who were created in the fourth heaven; they tried eating a cake, though ambrosia was their usual food; ambrosia was exhaled through the pores, but the cake made a new problem. They asked an angel to direct them to the W.C. "See that little globe down there?" he said. "That's the earth, the latrine of the universe." Man and woman hastened down, and have been here ever since.

I make a quick transition from the fourth heaven to Lord Bolingbroke. This writer, no doubt a great genius, gave Alexander Pope his theme of "all for the best"; it is to be found in Bolingbroke's posthumous work and recorded in Shaftesbury's *Characteristics of Men* in the *Treatise on Moralists*.

Bolingbroke, Shaftesbury, and Pope, their industrious amanuensis, resolve their general question no better than the rest. Their "all for the best" says no more than that immutable laws govern everything. We learn very little when we remark, after the manner of little children, that flies are created to be eaten by spiders, spiders by swallows, swallows by hawks, hawks by eagles, eagles by men, and men by one another, to be food for worms, and finally (at least one out of a thousand) prey for devils foreverlastingly.

There is a regular, recurring order of things for animals of all kinds. When a stone forms in my bladder, the mechanical process is wonderful: sandy particles come together, by the Newtonian law of attraction, and form a stone which gradually increases, according to the regular order of things, and gives me the most exquisite sensation of pain. A surgeon, cunning in the art of

Tubal Cain, cuts into me with a sharp instrument, severs the perineum, seizes the stone with his forceps (it breaks, during his labor, in the regular mechanical order of things), and in the same order of things I die in frightful torments. All this is "for the best," being in the obvious physical order of things; and I know as well as you do that I perish.

Were we insensitive, there would be nothing to say against this system of things; but that's not the point we're considering. We want to know if there aren't physical evils, and how they come to be. There is no absolute evil, says Pope in his *Essay on Man;* or, if there are particular evils, taken together they make up a general good. It is a strange general good which is made up of the stone and the gout, of all sorts of sufferings, and of death and damnation.

This system represents the Author of Nature as a powerful and malevolent monarch, who cares not a whit for the destruction of thousands of men, or for those who spend their days in penury and tears, so long as He carries out His designs.

Philosophers who embrace the doctrine that this is the best of all possible worlds are therefore far from a comfortable solution. The question of good and evil remains in obscurest chaos for those who seek to fathom it. Let us place at the end of every chapter of metaphysics the two letters used by Roman judges when they did not understand a plea: N. L., *non liquet,* not clear.

Passion

TELL me, doctor — I don't mean a doctor of medicine, who really has some degree of information, having dissected assiduously the human matrix to find something of how the thinking being is made; I mean a very different sort of person, a doctor of theology — tell me why it is that, your pretty young housekeeper having said a few endearing words and given herself coquettish airs, your blood warms up, your whole body tingles with desire, and you partake of pleasures whereby is introduced into the world another being all sodden with original sin?

Please explain how the act is connected with the result.

The next morning while you take your chocolate your memory recalls the pleasures of the

97

night, and the scene comes back with all its rapture. Have you any idea, my fine automaton, what this process of memory, possessed by you in common with all animals, really is?

I perceive, doctor, by the words you have been stammering out, that you do not know what the soul is, and that you have been talking all your life without a clear idea of it. If you don't know, why not acknowledge it like an honest man?

In his irritation the doctor becomes agitated; blood rushes to his face; if he had been stronger than I, and had not been restrained by a sense of decency, he would certainly have struck me. His heart swells; the systole and diastole fail in their regular operation; his brain is congested and he falls down in a fit of apoplexy. What connection can there be between the blood, heart, and brain, and an opinion contrary to your own? I utter certain sounds — he utters certain sounds — and he drops dead!

A guest sits at table enjoying the conversation and gaiety. A letter is handed him; he reads it and is overwhelmed with astonishment, grief, and fear. The peristaltic motion of his intestines becomes spasmodic, the sphincter of his rectum opens in the agitation of his muscles, and the unfortunate man, instead of finishing his dinner in comfort, sits befouled.

Tell me what connection nature sets up between shock and soiled breeches?

Poor puppets of the Eternal Artificer, who know neither why nor how the invisible hand pulls the strings, at length to pack us away in our wooden box!

We can only repeat with Aristotle, "All is hidden, all is secret."

Philosopher

THE philosopher is no emotionalist; he does not set himself up as a prophet; he does not represent himself to be inspired by the gods.

To the humility of the nations of the West, we must turn to the East to find a sage of simple manners, unassuming character, without arrogance and without sham, who taught men how to live happily six hundred years before the Christian era. That sage is Confucius.

What finer rules of conduct than his have been given us? "Rule a state as you rule a family. A man cannot govern his family well without furnishing a good example. Virtue should be possessed by the monarch and his man alike. Prevent crime; that saves the trouble of punishing it. Do to others as to yourself. Love mankind as a whole but cherish the good in particular. Forget injuries but never kindnesses."

The Greek philosophers later taught a morality equally pure. If they are still respected it is because they were just and because they taught mankind to be so.

When I speak of philosophers I do not refer to the crass and brutal cynics who ape Diogenes, but rather to those who follow Plato and Cicero. As for you, materialists, and you too, you men of petty mind invested with petty jobs and petty authority by a petty government, who exclaim against and abuse philosophy, continue so long as you please with your invective! You are Nomentanuses inveighing against Horace, Cotins yapping at Boileau!

99

The philosopher, a lover of wisdom and truth, avoids the senseless and the depraved. He should live in a society of philosophers. The sage should never hold forth among the unthinking; contrariwise, it has been said that he should be a madman with the mad, foolish with fools, even knavish with scoundrels. But that predicates his sharing the opinions of mankind's deluders. Would one ask a respectable physician to conform with the practices of charlatans?

When a countryman sees a snake ready to strike, he kills it; when a sage perceives a bigot and fanatic, what does he do? He prevents him from biting.

Plagiarism

WHEN an author sells the thoughts of another for his own, the larceny is called plagiarism. All the manufacturers of dictionaries, all compilers who do nothing but repeat the opinions, errors, impostures, and truths already written, we may term honest plagiarists — they do not pretend to invention. They merely sell in quarto what already exists in folio. Call them bookmakers but not authors; classify them as second-hand dealers, not plagiarists.

The most singular of all plagiarists was probably Father Barre, author of a ten-volume history of Germany. A history of Charles XII had just been printed, and he took more than two hundred pages of it for his own work, making his Duke of Lorraine say exactly what was said by Charles XII. A journalist, recognizing the extraordinary resemblance, blamed the plagiarism on the author of the history of Charles XII, who had written it twenty years before! Plagiarism flourishes especially in poetry. But of all larceny, this is certainly the least dangerous to society.

Post

IF a friend needs money in St. Petersburg and you are in Smyrna, you can rapidly send it to him by post. If your mistress is in Bordeaux and you are with your regiment before Prague, she can give you regular accounts of the constancy of her affection by letter; she can tell you all the news of the town save her own infidelities.

Some there are who send you by post a play written in a good round hand, complete with blank leaves on which you are requested kindly to make your critical observations; some regale you with the first volume of a work of metaphysical research, speedily to be followed by a second. They do not know what dangers they run. Why, every idle postmaster can learn where a bad playwright or metaphysician is to be found!

Property

"LIBERTY and property!" is the great national cry of the English. It is certainly better than "St. George and my right," or "St. Denis and Montjoie"; it is the cry of nature.

The idea of having property doubles a man's strength. He labors for himself and his family with more vigor and pleasure than he would for a master.

The slave who is in the power of another has little inclination for marriage; he shudders at the thought of producing slaves like himself. His industry is damped, his soul is deadened, and his powers are never exerted to the full. The possessor of property, on the contrary, desires a wife to share his happiness and children to assist in his labors. He aids in fostering commerce. He supplies his country soldiers.

All working men do not become rich, nor is it necessary that they be so. The state needs citizens who possess strength and happiness if nothing else. Even those without property can participate in the prosperity of the rest. They are free to dispose of their labor in the best market; this freedom is an effective substitute for property. The assurance of adequate wages supports their spirits; they bring up their families in their own useful occupations with success and even willingness. It is this class, so underestimated by the great and wealthy, that constitutes a nursery for soldiers.

Quack

PHYSICIANS cling to cities; there are few of them in country places. Cities contain rich citizens; their maladies spring from debauchery, gluttony, and excitements.

The famous physician Dumoulin said when dying, "I leave two great physicians behind me, simple food and pure water."

In 1728 a quack confided to some friends that his uncle, who had lived to the age of almost a hundred, and then had been killed by an accident, had left him the secret of a kind of water which would prolong life to one hundred and fifty, providing one lived sanely. When a funeral passed he would shrug and say, "Poor fellow, if he had only drunk my water!"

His friends who drank his water and followed his regimen found themselves in good health and praised its virtues. The quack then put it up in six-franc bottles and it sold prodigiously. It was nothing but Seine water with a pinch of salt in it, but those who made an effort at living sanely while they took it, and had good constitutions to begin with, soon found themselves cured of their indispositions.

Those who were not cured were told, "It's your own fault. Have you been temperate? Have you been continent? You see!"

When it was found out that it was only Seine water, people naturally took no more of it and resorted to other quacks. But he must be credited with doing no little good — he advised men to temperance. He just charged too much for the water.

I knew a London physician named Brown who had managed a sugar plantation in the Barbadoes. He found that some money had been stolen. So he called all the Negro workers together and said, "Last night a great serpent appeared to me in a dream. It told me that the thief who stole my money would have a parrot's feather at the end of his nose right now!"

The guilty man rubbed his nose and was detected. This kind of quackery is scarcely to be condemned.

Mohamet was upon the point of failure when the Arabs of Medina were persuaded that he was an intimate friend of the archangel Gabriel. To-day if anybody in Constantinople should suggest that he was on amicable terms with Raphael, an archangel of even higher rank, he would risk public empaling.

Quacks should know their time.

There has been something of the quack about every founder of a school of philosophy, but the greatest quacks of all were those who aspired to rule. Cromwell, an excellent example of the kind, appeared precisely at the right time to succeed. Under Elizabeth he would have been hung, under Charles II, laughed at. Fortunately for him he came at a time when the English were fed up with royalty. His son followed him when they were fed up with protectors.

Another sort of quack is that unhappy class which writes for a livelihood. A poor man without a trade, who has had the misfortune of being at college, and so thinks he knows how to write, will go to a publisher and ask for work. The publisher, knowing that householders have bookshelves which must be filled, will give him a history to abridge or an anthology to make. He will order a collection of *bon-mots* or a biographical dictionary in which the writer places obscure pedants beside Cicero and sonneteers next to Virgil.

Other publishers may require translations of novels or a four-hundred-page omnibus. Still others will hand a file of newspaper clippings to some genius, enjoining him to bring it back in three months as *A History of the Times* by a Personage High in the Government.

This quackery goes on and on, like nostrums to whiten the skin and blacken the hair.

Queries

WHY was not a tenth of the money lost in the war of 1741 used in helping and improving the country? If half the men killed to no purpose in Germany had lived, might not the state have been more flourishing? Why prefer a war to the happy labors of peace?

Why have nations reduced to extremity and humiliation still supported themselves in spite of all efforts to crush them? Is it not because they were active and industrious? Are not their people like bees: you take their honey and they work to produce more?

Why in pagan antiquity were there no theological disputes, or groups divided into hostile sects?

Why do booksellers publicly display the *Course of Atheism* by Lucretius, why is it to be found, in handsome morocco, in the libraries of princes and bishops, while the works of modern deists are banned?

Why do we abandon to sneers and neglect that great mass of men who cultivate the earth that we may eat of its fruits, while we pay court to the useless men who live by their labor?

Why is there no place on earth where there are not more insects than men?

Why, since we are always complaining of our ills, are we always doing something to redouble them? Why, since we are so miserable, is it thought that to die is bad — when it is perfectly clear that not to have been alive, before birth, was not bad?

Why do we exist? In fact, why does anything exist?

Right

AT the time when France went wild over the system of Law, a man (who was always right) came to the controller-general who was then in office and said:

"Sir, you are completely mad. You think that we can increase the national wealth by printing paper money. This is not wealth, but only a sham for the real wealth of produce and manufacture. What you should have increased was our production of grain, wine, linen, and so forth, making sure that it found a market. But you make ten times as much in paper notes as we have actual wealth in money and goods; you are ten times mad."

No sooner had he finished than he was conducted to the lock-up of St. Lazarus. After a period during which he had plenty of time to improve his sense of the rightness of things, he was released. Thereupon he went straight to Rome and demanded a public audience so that he might not be interrupted. This is how he addressed the pope:

"Holy Father, you do everything contrariwise to the way Christ instructed. He was poor and you are very rich. He paid tribute and you exact it. He submitted to the powers that be and you have become one of them. He wandered on foot and you visit Castle Gandolfo in a splendid carriage. He ate whatever people gave him; you would have us eat fish on Fridays even though we reside far from rivers or the sea. I revere you, however, for everything else you do, so please give me an indulgence."

When he was at last released from the Castle St. Angelo he proceeded to Venice and asked an audience with the doge.

"Your serenity," he began, "don't you look pretty foolish, marrying the sea every year? In the first place, people have to marry the same person only once; in the second, your marriage is only half performed, like Harlequin's, because it lacks the consent of one of the parties; in the third, one of these days the other maritime powers will ridicule you for being unable to consummate the marriage."

After a stay under the leads of the doge's palace he was let out and proceeded to Constantinople, where he obtained an interview with the mufti and thus addressed him:

"Your religion has some good points, such as the worship of the Supreme Being, and the obligation of being just and charitable, but it is really nothing more than a hash of Judaism mixed with Mother Goose rhymes. If the archangel Gabriel had actually brought the leaves of the Koran to Mahomet, in all of Arabia someone would have seen him, whereas nobody did. Mahomet was therefore a big impostor, who deceived poor ignorant people." He had scarcely finished the last word before he was impaled. Nevertheless he had been right all along.

Self-Love

A BEGGAR in Madrid was asking alms; a passer-by said to him, "Aren't you ashamed to beg like this, when you can work?" "Sir," replied the mendicant, "I ask you for money, not advice," and he turned his back with true Castilian dignity. The beggar was haughty; his vanity was easily wounded; he asked alms out of self-love, and would not suffer reprimand out of even greater self-love.

A missionary in India saw a fakir loaded with chains, naked as an ape, lying on his belly and lashing himself for the sins of his fellows, who gave him coins. "What self-renouncement!" said a spectator. "Self-renouncement!" repeated the fakir scornfully, "I lash myself in this world only to serve you the same in the next, when you will be the horse and I the rider."

Whoever said that self-love is the basis of all our emotions and actions was right; it isn't necessary to prove that men have faces, nor that they possess self-love. It is the instrument of our preservation: it is like a provision for perpetuating mankind; it is essential, it is dear to us, it is delightful, and it should be hidden.

Slavery

WHEN I was at my country place at Mount Krapak I read a book full of wit and paradox in the manner of Montesquieu, against whom, as a matter of fact, it was written, which maintained that slavery is to be preferred to free labor. Pity those unhappy free men, it said, who must earn their livelihood where they can! No one has the responsibility of looking after them or feeding them, whereas slaves are fed and sheltered like horses by their masters. True enough; but human beings prefer to provide for themselves, and horses bred in freedom need no stables.

The book justly remarks that workmen lose many days when they cannot work — but this is not because they are independent, but because of ridiculous hindrances put between them and their production. It asserts, again with truth, that princes enfranchised their serfs through avarice. To get the money laboriously amassed by these unhappy souls they signed their letters of manumission. They did not bestow liberty, they sold it. Emperor Henry V began it by freeing the serfs of Spires and Worms in the twelfth century. The kings of France followed his example. Nothing tends more to prove the value of liberty than the high price these laboring men paid for it.

It is really for the man most affected to decide what state he prefers. Ask the humblest toiler, ragged, with only a crust of black bread, a bed of straw, and a hut half open to the elements, whether he would rather be a slave, better fed, clothed, and bedded. He will recoil with horror at the proposal.

Slow-Bellies

ST. PAUL says that the Cretans were all liars, evil beasts, and slow-bellies. Dr. Hequet understood by this that they were constipated. If they were, they were doubtless more prone to choler than not. When you want to ask a favor, make sure first of the state of stomach of the person you would approach. We all know that character and disposition are directly influenced by the bowels. Cardinel Richelieu had the piles, which explains a lot about him. Anne of Austria always called him *cul pourri*, "sore bottom"—enough to redouble his bile; it may have cost Marshal Marillac his life and Marshal Bassompierre his liberty.

I am inclined to believe that by slow-bellies St. Paul meant voluptuaries and gross feeders, the sort of rich-prelate people who lay abed all morning to recover from the excesses of the night before. People may, of course, lie abed all morning without being liars or evil beasts. People who do are generally stored with social graces and relaxed in their dealings with the world.

I regret that St. Paul should have tried to offend a whole island. Nothing was gained by calling everybody on it an evil beast; doubtless men of merit were to be found in Crete. Perhaps St. Paul was the difficult one to live with, the proud spirit and imperious character. He boasted of being a Roman citizen born at Tarsus, whereas St. Jerome considered him a poor provincial Jew born at Giscala in Galilee. In his letters he always spoke magisterially: "I will come," he informs the Corinthians, "and I will judge of you all on the testimony of two or three witnesses; and I will pardon neither those who have sinned, nor others." A little severe, that "nor others."

Returning to my text of slow-bellies, I would advise all missionaries never to start their work among any people with insults.

I do not of course regard the Cretans as the most just and respectable of men, as they were once called. I make no attempt to reconcile their virtue with the simulated bull of which the lovely Pasiphae was enamored, nor with the skill of Daedalus in constructing it so that she was enabled to produce the Minotaur, to which the pious Minos sacrificed seven youths and virgins of Athens every year.

As for the poor Greeks and Jews who now inhabit the steep mountains of this island, among them there may possibly be liars and evil beasts, but I have no information as to their digestion. All that I can hope is that they have enough to eat.

Taste

TASTE, the sense by which we distinguish flavor, is used metaphorically as the sense whereby we distinguish beauty and defects in the arts. As an epicure quickly perceives the liquors in a mixture, a man of taste, or connoisseur, at a single glance takes in a mixture of styles or of good and bad. Bad taste in food likes high seasoning and exotic dishes; in art, excessive ornament and strained effects. Depraved taste is gratification with what should disgust; it is a sort of disease. To prefer burlesque to the noble, affectation to the natural, is a mental disease. A taste for the arts requires more cultivation than a taste for food; we more often finish by liking what at first we detested.

In many matters taste is arbitrary, as in clothing, interior decoration, or equipages — though these scarcely belong to the fine arts. It is fancy rather than taste which produces so many new fashions. In a nation taste may become vitiated after a period of excellence. Fearing the charge of imitation, artists seek novel and devious means of avoiding the natural which their predecessors cultivated to advantage. If there is merit in their work, it conceals their defects, and the sensation-loving public runs after them, grows bored, and turns to even lesser efforts in which nature is further abandoned. As an artist forms his taste by degrees, so does a nation. It is shadowed long in barbarism, then rises feebly till a noon occurs, after which it declines into sad twilight.

Testicles

THE etymology of this word is obscure; it seems to mean *little witnesses*. Sixtus V, in his letter of 25 June 1587 to his nuncio in Spain, ordered him to unmarry all who were not possessed of testicles, by which order (executed by Philip II) it seems that there were many Spanish husbands lacking these organs.

A prejudice has long been entertained in the Russian Church that it is not lawful to say mass without testicles; at least they must be somewhere about the officiator, say in his pocket. This idea originated at the Council of Nice, which forbade admission into orders of any who were mutilated.

The example of Origen, and of certain enthusiasts who had emasculated themselves, gave cause for the edict, which was reiterated at the Council of Arles.

The Greek Church did not bar from the altar those who had undergone the operation of Origen against their consent. The patriarchs of Constantinople: Nicetas, Ignatius, Photius, and Methodius were eunuchs. This point of discipline seems undecided, at the time of my writing, in the Catholic Church. It appears that a eunuch would require a dispensation to become ordained as a priest. Exclusion of eunuchs from the altar is paradoxical, as the service exacts purity and chastity; such priests would certainly be tempted less in having to confess pretty girls.

A word or two on hermaphrodites. Can a creature possess testicles and ovaries at the same time? Can a hermaphrodite become pregnant? There are insects with both sexes; may not human beings be similarly endowed? How many things there are about man which are unknown or open to doubt! From his thoughts to his feelings and his spark of life, how much we discuss without really knowing the first thing about him!

Theatre

THERE was a time when the kings of France were excommunicated; kings of England likewise received their favors from the court of Rome; then the representatives of kings were excommunicated — not their ambassadors, but their players, who are kings and emperors three or four times a week, and rule the world to eke out a living.

Because of this there were many victims, notably Alexander, Caesar, Athalie, Polyeucte, Andromache, Brutus, Zaire, and Harlequin.

The reason for this action against them was that these ladies and gentlemen represented the passions; but if interpreting the human heart merits so severe a punishment, an even greater rigor should be shown painters and sculptors. Licentious pictures are publicly sold; Titian and Correggio represent Venus quite naked, a danger to impressionable youth; but players do no more than recite the admirable lines of *Cinna* for a couple of hours. Why are the living interpretations on the stage condemned when those on canvas are not? What would Sophocles and Euripides have said if they could have foreseen that a people who ceased to be barbarous only by imitating them, would one day inflict this upon the stage which in their time received such honor?

Rome, from whom we learned our catechism, does not use it as we do; she has always known how to temper her laws according to the time and the occasion. She has known how to distinguish impudent mountebanks, who were rightly censured, from the scholarly players who helped revive tragedy. Even today comedies are played in religious houses in Rome. Ladies go to them without scandal. Speeches recited from the boards are not deemed diabolical. We have even seen *George Dandin* performed in Rome by nuns, before an audience including ladies and ecclesiastics. The wise Romans are particularly careful how they excommunicate the gentlemen who sing soprano in the opera, for it is bad enough to be castrated in this world without being damned in the other.

St. Thomas Aquinas, who never really saw a good play or company of players, thought that the theatre might be useful. He had good sense and justice enough to recognize the virtues of the art, unfinished as it was when he knew it, and to permit and approve it. St. Charles Borromeo personally examined the pieces which were played at Milan, and gave them his approval by signature. Who can now be such a Visigoth as to treat Roderigo and Chimene as corruptors of the soul? Would that the barbarous enemies of the art had the piety of Polyeucte, the clemency of Augustus, the virtue of Burrhus, and would die like the husband of Alzira!

Usages

NATIONS should not be judged by their usages and popular superstitions. Had Caesar, in the interest of promoting Roman commerce, sent ambassadors to China, the emperor Yventi who then reigned in China, and who is represented in the annals as a wise and scholarly prince, after receiving them with all Chinese politeness, would have informed himself secretly of the usages, sciences, and religion of the Romans. His advisor would have told him that their priests counted years in so absurd a manner that the sun was already in the spring solstice when the Romans were celebrating the first feasts of winter; that a college of abracadabra was supported at great expense to tell just when to start on a journey or fight a battle, which was found by inspecting a bullock's liver or watching how a chicken pecked its grain; and that, although the people worshipped a supreme and only deity, they also had many others — the good women having little household gods, *penates,* four or five inches high, including a goddess of bosoms and another of posteriors. But instead of laughing at all this, Yventi, being as just as he was polite, would have asked the ambassadors questions, and would have learned that Caesar had recently reformed the calendar, and that the college of augurs was a survival of barbarous times, which Caesar never consulted — in fact, Cicero, a great orator and philosopher, had written a book against it, called *Of Divination.* The emperor would have been given the book, read it with the aid of a translator, and been moved to admiration not only of the work but of the Roman republic.

Verse

It is easier to write prose than poetry. More than one prose writer has affected to despise poetry. Montaigne made the quip, "If you can't attain poetry, get your revenge by writing bad verses." Montesquieu, falling down as a poet, professed to find no merit in Virgil or Horace.

I believe that no truly expressive man has failed to love poetry. I need cite only Caesar and Cicero; one wrote a tragedy on Oedipus, and we have fragments of the other which rank with the best that preceded Lucretius, Virgil, and Horace. The Abbé Trublet, whoever he is, wrote somewhere that he couldn't read a single poem through. Really? Then what can we read through, what can we understand or peruse with uninterrupted pleasure, any more than poetry?

116

Virtue

SUPPOSE that a hermit be gluttonous, drunken, and given over to self-debauch; he is vicious. Or say that if he has contrary qualities he be virtuous. I cannot agree to this. He is vile if he has the faults mentioned, but he is not vicious, wicked, or punishable by society, for his infamies do it no harm. It may be presumed that if he were to re-enter society he would not adorn it; he would indeed be wicked. And it is certain that the other hermit, the temperate and chaste one, would be a good man; for in society faults augment and good qualities diminish.

Nero, Pope Alexander VI, and other monsters of the kind have done good deeds. If they did, they were virtuous at the time. Certain theologians have said that the divine Marcus Aurelius was not virtuous, that he was a misled stoic who, not content with commanding men, would be esteemed by them besides; that he gave himself credit for the good which he did mankind; that all his life he was just, industrious, and beneficent through vanity; that he only deceived men by his virtues. To this I exclaim, O Lord, let us have more such sinners!

War

ALL animals are forever warring; each kind is born to devour another. Not even the gentle sheep and dove fail to take life in eating, if you consider the tiny organisms that inhabit a blade of grass or husk of seed. Males fight each other for females, like Menelaus and Paris. Air, land, and sea are theatres of unceasing combat.

God has given reason to man; using it, he should scorn to debase himself by aping animals, especially since he has neither natural equipment for killing nor instinct for sucking blood.

None will disagree that war brings pestilence and famine in its wake, after seeing the hospitals of the German army, or the villages in which some great exploit of war has taken place.

Doubtless it is a fine art which desolates countries, destroys habitations, and causes the death of hundreds of thousands. It was first cultivated by nations banded together for their common good; the Greek confederation set out in a myriad ships for the Phrygian confederation to exterminate it if it could. The Roman people, in solemn conclave, voted that it was to their interest to attack the Veii or the Volscians. It is no different today.

Peoples fall upon one another, not only without personal interest in the affair, but without knowing what it is all about. Five or six belligerent powers, three against three, two against four, or one against five, all detesting one another, unite and attack by turns; the only point of agreement is to do as much harm as possible.

The most wonderful part of the infernal business is that each leader of murderers causes his colors to be blessed and, before setting out on carnage, piously invokes God. If a leader kills only a couple of thousand he renders no thanks to God for so small a favor, but when he has wiped out ten thousand by fire and sword, and levelled a town to the ground, he bursts out into a paean of thanksgiving. Orators are paid to celebrate the slaughter, holding forth for a long time, and citing historic precedents from ancient Palestine. When they have no victory to eulogize they fill in their time declaiming against vices: they show that women who put carmine on their cheeks will be consumed in red fire, that certain plays are works of the devil, and that men who pay ninety cents a pound for fresh fish during Lent will work their salvation, while other good folk who can afford to eat only hamburger will go to perdition.

Miserable physicians of the soul, for an hour and a half you hold forth on pin-pricks, but utter never so much as a word about the malady which decimates us! Philosophers, moralists, burn your books! While the whim of a few men makes heroes of those who loyally murder, can you ply your trades?

What's the use of humanity, beneficence, modesty, temperance, mildness, wisdom, and piety if a couple of ounces of lead go through me and I die at the age of twenty in inexpressible torments, amidst a thousand of my dying comrades, while my eyes open for the last time on the sight of the town where I was born going up in flames, and my ears hear as their last sound the cries of women and children perishing under the ruins? And all for the interest of some man I do not even know!

Montesquieu has said, "Self-defence sometimes dictates aggression. If one people takes advantage of peace to put itself in a position to destroy another, immediate attack on the first is the only means of preventing such destruction."

How can a peace-time attack prevent destruction? You must be certain that the neighbor will destroy you if he becomes powerful. To be certain you must see that he is all ready for your overthrow, in which case it is he who commences the war. What you propose is the most unjust of wars: it will kill your neighbor, before he attacks you, just in case he might do so. To risk the ruin of your country in the hope of ruining that of another without reason is certainly neither honest nor useful; for success is never assured, as you well know.

If your neighbor seems to become too powerful in peace time, what stops you from making yourself equally powerful? If he makes alliances, you can make them too. If his people are made up of fewer monks and more soldiers and manufacturers than yours, you can imitate him in his prudent economy. If he uses his sailors to better advantage, employ yours in the same manner. That is fair enough. But to expose your people to the most abject of misery in the false ambition of overturning your brother the neighboring ruler—certainly you'll get no advice to do so from the president of any peaceable society.

Patan," he goes on to observe, "is so great that the men are constrained to adopt certain garniture in order to be safe from their amorous enterprises."

Montesquieu was assuredly never at Patan. He got it from travelers who either were misled themselves or wished to mislead others. Let us try to be a little more exact, finding truth by observation, not report.

Ben Abul Kiba, in his *Mirror of the Faithful*, relates that one of the viziers of the great Solyman addressed the following tirade to an envoy of Charles V: "Christian dog — for whom I have, however, a special esteem — do you reproach me with having four wives, according to our holy laws, while you empty a dozen barrels a year and I do not touch a single glass of wine? What do you accomplish by passing more hours at table than I do in bed? I may get four children a year for the service of my august master, while you can scarcely produce one, so befuddled are you. And what would you have me do while a couple of my wives are far gone with child? Not attend to the other two, as my law commands? As for you, what do you do during your wife's lyings-in? Either you must rest idle or repair to another woman. You balance on a narrow bridge between two mortal sins, and must soon fall headlong into the pit of hell.

"Suppose that in our wars against you Christian dogs we lose a hundred thousand soldiers. There we have, right off, a hundred thousand girls to provide for. Is it not for the wealthy to care for them? Evil betide any Mussulman so cold-hearted as not to take in four pretty girls as his legitimate wives, and to treat them as they

123

merit! In your country what of the trumpeter of dawn, the cock; of the ram, leader of his flock; of the bull, sovereign of the heifers—has not every one of them his seraglio? My conduct is restrained, considering Solomon's. Cease to accuse a sage of indulgence when he is content with so moderate a repast. I permit you to drink; allow me to love. You may change your wines; let me change my women."

"Dog of a Mussulman," replied the German, "for whom I have, however, a profound veneration, may I refute your arguments? If you have four wives you have four harpies, always backbiting, vexing, and fighting among themselves. Your house is a den of discord; none of them can love you, for each has only a quarter of you, and can bestow only a quarter of her heart in return. None of them can serve to make your life agreeable. They are prisoners. You are their absolute master and therefore they hate you. You are forced to guard them with eunuchs, who whip them when they are too happy. You compare yourself to a cock; a cock never has his pullets whipped by a capon. Pattern yourself as much as you want after animals; for my part, I want to love like a man. As for wine, it may be evil to drink in Arabia, but in Germany it is praiseworthy!"

Xenophanes

BAYLE made this heading a pretext for writing a panegyric on the devil, as Simonides once took the occasion of a wrestler winning in the Olympic games to compose an ode in praise of Castor and Pollux.

What do the reveries of Xenophanes matter to us? What's the point of knowing that he thought nature an infinite, innate mass composed of tiny particles, or that his ideas were very much like the later Spinoza's, even in the feature of contradicting himself frequently?

O philosophers, *my* sage is the miller in his windmill, who turns his sails to the breeze, puts my grain into his hopper, and grinds it into meal for me and my family. My sage is the weaver who, with his shuttle, makes figures of linen or silk to cover my walls with fine colors. Or he is the watchmaker who gives me a chronometer of silver or gold to put into my pocket.

Yvetot

THIS is the name of a town in France, six leagues from Rouen in Normandy, which has long laid claim to the title of a kingdom, according to Robert Gaguin the sixteenth-century historian. I say quite a little about it, to make a decent entry under the letter Y, but my translator has deleted it all because it is theological stuff, grown dull today.

Zeal

IN religion this is a pure and enlightened attachment to worship of the Divinity and its maintenance and progress; but when it grows blind and false and takes to persecution, it becomes the greatest scourge of humanity. It is chilling to observe how many abuses and dissentions arose from the deep ignorance in which Europe was so long plunged. Those leaders who are aware of the importance of enlightenment become the benefactors of mankind in encouraging the dissemination of knowledge, which is the basis for the peace and happiness of the world, and the surest bulwark against the mischief of fanaticism.

AUTHORS' & PRINTER'S NOTE:

Our errors not proceeding from malice, but being the natural consequence of human weakness, we hope we shall be pardoned for them both in this world and the next.

Given at Mount Krapak, the 30 of Janus, in the year of the world according to

Scaliger	5,022
Les Etrennes Mignonnes	5,776
Riccioli	5,956
Eusebius	6,972
The Alphosine Tables	8,707
The Egyptians	370,000
The Chaldaeans	465,102
The Brahmins	780,000
The Philosophers	*Infinity*

and printed at Mount Vernon, in the Baskerville types, on paper made especially for the Peter Pauper Press.